MUSHROOM COOKBOOK

MUSHROOM COOKBOOK

Recipes for White & Exotic Varieties

MIMI BRODEUR

STACKPOLE
BOOKS

Printed in the United States

10 9 8 7 6 5 4 3 2 1

FIRST EDITION

Design by Beth Oberholtzer

Library of Congress Cataloging-in-Publication Data

Brodeur, Mimi.
  Mushroom cookbook : recipes for white and exotic varieties / Mimi Brodeur
    p.   cm.
  Includes bibliographical references and index.
  ISBN 0-8117-3274-6 (hardcover)
  1. Cookery (Mushrooms)   I. Title.
TX804.B76   2005
641.6′58–dc22   2004025659
ISBN 978-0-8117-3274-1

To my dear Rick, Andrew,
Ellen, Nikki, and Liza

For never picking out the mushrooms
when the meal was served.

Contents

Side Dishes

Build-Ons and Add-Ons

Preface

Why don't you write a book about mushrooms? The idea was simple enough, the topic vast, and the starring fungi diverse and enjoyable. But what do I know about mushrooms other than that I like eating them?

I know what cooking methods work best with each variety, and living in Pennsylvania, one of the top mushroom-producing states, I have a myriad of cultivated mushrooms at my fingertips. With my background of writing food articles, reviewing restaurants, and developing recipes, as well as a grand diplome from LaVarenne cooking school in Paris, why not familiarize people with all those weird and wonderful varieties of mushrooms cropping up at grocery stores and farmers' markets?

Everyone's familiar with the omnipresent white mushroom. It has the flexibility of an Olympic gymnast, showing up in a variety of cooking routines, alone or paired with perfect partners. These smooth, white-capped mushrooms, which can vary in size from button to jumbo to stuffer, lend themselves to various cooking needs.

White mushrooms glamorized the 1950s, their smooth, sleek caps sliced and served sautéed with onions over thick steaks and chops, as crudités on dip platters, or smothered in sour cream sauce and blanketed over chicken breasts. The widespread appeal of mushrooms continues to be their diversity and adaptability to just about any cooking process.

Using mushrooms to enhance the texture and flavor of recipes is as easy as slipping handfuls of slices into sauces, tossing them into stir-fries, or folding them into potato or egg dishes. Roasting and grilling mushrooms releases their nuttier, earthy characteristics, adding a different flavor to main courses or side dishes.

When I first started experimenting with various types of mushrooms, I found that I could easily mix different varieties, such as portabellas and shiitakes, royal trumpets and oyster mushrooms, criminis and white mushrooms. In fact, mushroom combinations are now offered in $\frac{1}{4}$- and $\frac{1}{2}$-pound packages at the supermarket. Specialty mushrooms may be substituted for white mushrooms in most recipes. You can keep costs down by using the cheaper white mushrooms in large part, supplemented by meatier, more flavor-penetrating exotic types.

In a little over two decades, there has been an explosion of mushroom types available in groceries. This cookbook focuses on those that are readily available year-round. Many kinds of mushrooms that once were available only by foraging in the wild are now being cultivated. With many varieties of wild mushrooms being poisonous, it's best to leave foraging to the experts and do your hunting in the comfort of the produce aisles.

In some areas, freshly picked wild mushrooms may turn up at local farmers' markets, at specialty gourmet food stores, and in the produce section at peak harvest times throughout the year. Take advantage of these fresh wild finds appearing with gusto during their peak season. Two of the most prolific hand-picked wild mushroom varieties are morels and chanterelles. They are also available year-round at specialty food shops and via mushroom-growing houses, either flash-frozen or dried. You may certainly substitute wild mushrooms for cultivated varieties in the recipes in this book.

For people living in parts of the country lacking in mushroom diversity, the Sources section at the back of this book lists specialty mushroom companies with numerous mushroom types available by mail order.

By learning more about each of the most prevalent mushrooms available, preparation and preferred cooking methods become evident. Most mushroom varieties don't taste exceptional eaten in their raw state, except for the white, enoki, and beech varieties. Portabellas and shiitakes are excellent grilled, and pom pom mushrooms are at their best when sautéed with butter, garlic, and wine. By bringing home and trying different mushroom types, you'll soon become familiar with what cooking methods and ingredients work well together.

In the following pages, I describe a dozen or so of the most readily available mushroom types. There are many different varieties of mushrooms to choose from, but I have set my recipe sights on those most accessible to the home cook. These include the most prevalent white and specialty varieties, as well as some notable wild mushrooms that may be stocked in the supermarket produce section when available.

These pages are filled with comforting bistro-style recipes, both homey and gourmet, nurturing soul-soaking foods that will help you cure the blues, laugh off a bad date, or add an extra special note to an already good day. Come along with me as we play around in the kitchen and unearth the musty scent of newfound fungi. Some recipes are meant for cooks who love to poke around in the kitchen, others are quick to prepare, and many offer time-saving shortcuts and substitutions.

I wish to thank Kyle Weaver, editor, and Amy Cooper, associate editor at Stackpole Books; Jim Angelucci, general manager at Phillips Mushroom Farms for his wealth of mushroom knowledge; Mushroom Information Center; Mike Reed at Country Fresh Mushroom Company; Laura Bachman, for all of her recipe testing and feedback; Bernadette Bream, for her help in scouting out mushroom country; and Ruth and Mike Brodeur, for their continuous culinary support.

All about Mushrooms

Historical accounts and legends depicted mushrooms as having unique spiritual, medicinal, and epicurean powers, and Asian cultures have long believed in their healing and protective qualities. Modern research suggests that certain varieties of mushrooms may indeed protect against some types of cancer and illnesses. Oyster mushrooms have been proven to lower cholesterol and triglycerol levels. Shiitake mushrooms appear to improve the body's immune system and blood-clotting abilities.

Nutritionally, mushrooms provide important minerals and contain beneficial amounts of potassium and B vitamins, such as riboflavin and niacin. They have less than 30 calories per quarter pound and are low in fat and cholesterol.

Once reserved for royalty and nobility in ancient Rome and Egypt, the prolific mushroom has trickled down to the common man's plate and palate. The extravagant sun king, Louis XIV, was noted by historians as one of the first to implement cultivators of white mushrooms. Grown in caves around Paris, these *champignons de Paris* were ancestors of our present-day white mushrooms *(Agaricus bisporus)*. Louis, like his mushroom connoisseur predecessors, appreciated the distinctive flavor and unique qualities of mushrooms. Later in the nineteenth century, these cultivation practices were introduced to England, which became proficient in the production of spawn, the fruit bodies of emerging fungi. The United States came to heavily rely upon this imported spawn until the turn of the twentieth century.

In 1891, William Falconer jolted enthusiasm for mushroom cultivation among gardeners, farmers, and especially florists when he published the first how-to book, titled *Mushrooms: How to Grow Them: A Practical Treatise on Mushroom Culture for Profit and Pleasure.* By 1903, thanks to advancements made by scientists at the American Spawn Company, the United States produced its own laboratory-cultured virgin spawn. By 1930, improved spawn quality, advances in growing mediums (pasteurized manure, sawdust, peat moss), and specialized mushroom cultivation houses were key factors in the rise of the seasonless mushroom industry in the United States. Pockets of backyard mushroom cultivators also sprang up across the country. At this time, Chester County, Pennsylvania, became the leading mushroom-growing area in the United States. Mushrooms still top the agricultural list in production in this state.

Today mushroom cultivation is evident in every state in the country, of which Pennsylvania ranks as the top producer, providing more than half the total U.S. production.

A Visit to Mushroom Country

It was serendipity that Pennsylvania became the top mushroom producer in the United States. If it hadn't been for florists messing around with spawn and smelly compost over a hundred years ago, I wouldn't be sitting at my desk in south-central Pennsylvania writing about these quirky, capped flukes of nature. Living an hour and a half away from innumerable mushroom farms, it was with erroneous preconceived notions about growing mushrooms that I drove to Kennett Square in Chester County to discover the truth.

Hints that mushroom country was fast approaching were sprinkled along Route 41. Handwritten signs reading, "Fresh Mushrooms Here," popped up on country groceries and roadside stands amid vast stretches of farmland and spurts of development. The air became thick with a pungent, hold-your-nose smell.

Kennett Square, deemed the mushroom capital of the world, is just about as southeastern as you can go in Pennsylvania without ending up in Delaware. It's a sleepy, blink-of-an-eye town consisting of hilly, narrow streets with tight-knit rows of small shops and eateries. Kennett Square maintains its historic presence without having become overly touristy or yuppified. In fact, once in town, you see no more blatant suggestions that this place is the center of the mushroom world. It has no visitors center, and the mushroom museum closed a few years ago. The locals told me that if I wanted to learn more about mushrooms, I should come back for the annual Mushroom Festival at the beginning of September. Mushroom farm tours may be arranged by appointment only.

It was in this town back in the late 1800s that florists began cultivating small crops of mushrooms amid flowers and plants in their humid, environmentally controlled greenhouses. This lower corner of Pennsylvania turned out to be an ideal setting for growing mushrooms. Growing houses solely for mushroom cultivation began springing up in Chester County at this time. Production of white or button mushrooms proliferated in this area, as well as other portions of Pennsylvania, such as Butler County north of Pittsburgh, because of the availability of ample growing materials (compost made from manure from surrounding farms and racetracks) and the proximity to major cities, which yielded immigrant labor (largely Italian) and laboratory-produced spawn accessibility.

When visiting these ongoing mushrooms farms around Kennett Square and Avondale, I was dressed inappropriately in T-shirt, jeans, and hiking boots. Modern-day mushroom farms consist of sterile, agriculturally composted beds, with bottles and bags of spawn suspended over hosed-down cement flooring. What I really needed was an umbrella and a clothespin for my nose for these regulated, humidity-controlled rooms dripping with condensation and reeking of moist sawdust, compost, and musty earth scents.

Mushroom farms are measured in square footage rather than acreage. These specialty farms look like army barracks lined with numerous bunkers. Some outpost buildings are prototype greenhouses made from insulated steel panels. These are specifically designed to create a myriad of growing environments for the different varieties of cultivated specialty and white mushrooms. Outside the growing houses were steamy mounds of racetrack and farm manure, which later would be pasteurized into sterile compost, a must-have ingredient in the production and proliferation of the Agaricus mushroom family: whites, criminis, and portabellas.

Some of the specially designed bunkers housed mind-boggling amounts of fruiting spawn, suspended from what look like plastic leaf bags covered with emerging yellow and gray oyster mushrooms.

These mushrooms grow out of tiny slits in suspended bags that control proliferation. In another environmentally controlled room, enoki and beech mushrooms sprouted from the tops of sterilized bottles.

Donning sanitary headwear, I stepped into one of the more traditional-looking buildings, constructed from cinder blocks. The room appeared to be filled with bunk beds of protruding dark mushroom caps. Emerging criminis, or brown mushrooms, were at different stages of development, varying in size and shape, which allowed for alternating crops of production. When left to grow for several days longer, criminis will mature into large, capped portabella mushrooms with exposed gills. After all mushrooms have been handpicked, new growing material is put in place and these beds are reused.

Portabella mushrooms ready to be picked.

Mushroom Varieties

Out of all the mushroom varieties, the portabella sparked the leap from the old familiar white or button mushrooms to the exotic mushroom world we enjoy today. Heavily marketed in the 1980s, portabellas and shiitakes began to emerge regularly on restaurant menus and supermarket shelves. Once considered expensive and gourmet, these varieties are as common now at grocery stores as their white mushroom cousins. *Specialty* is the term commonly used by the marketing industry to describe cultivated, non-white mushrooms. They are sometimes also called "exotics", but the most common term is specialty mushrooms. Many restaurants will use the term "wild mushrooms" on their menus. True wild mushrooms, however, are those varieties such as morels and chanterelles foraged in natural growing environments. Wild mushrooms should not be confused with those varieties that are cultivated in growing houses.

Specialty mushrooms are becoming increasing available and affordable to consumers. Man-made oak-sawdust logs have trimmed back the natural growing duration of shiitakes from several years to several months. Pom Pom mushrooms also are now being cultivated in growing houses though they are not as prominent as other mushroom varieties. Mail order, improved shipping distribution, and refined drying techniques have made other wild mushrooms and truffles more accessible as well. The price of specialty mushrooms has been coming down as growing and storage processes have improved, allowing everyone to enjoy their wide range of textures and flavors.

White Mushrooms *(Agaricus bisporus)*

These mushrooms are the most popular and predominant in the United States today. They are the staple of the mushroom crop, representing 90 percent of the consumer market. Labeled as white, button, jumbo, or stuffer, these mushrooms are conveniently sorted and graded according to cap size.

PURCHASING

White caps and stems should be free from bruising and blemishes, and the white, silky veils covering up dark gills should be intact. Mature mushrooms lose their moisture content, and thus the thin white skin

White mushrooms range from button to jumbo according to cap size.

or veil tends to withdraw from the stem, exposing dark, inky gills. These older mushrooms are still usable, but their distinct earthy flavor becomes more pronounced and intense. For longer shelf life, avoid mushrooms past their prime, marked by brown specks or exposed gills.

PUTTING AWAY

Fresh, firm white mushrooms will keep up to one week in the refrigerator. Store in breathable containers (not plastic bags) or in paper bags in the lower third of the refrigerator for better air circulation. Don't store mushrooms next to anything strong-smelling—they tend to absorb odors.

TO CLEAN

Wipe mushrooms with damp paper towels. If this method is a little too tedious, wash under cold, running water and dry spread out on a tea towel. Mushrooms should be washed right before use, or their texture will break down and their flesh will become soft and mottled looking. Lemon juice sprinkled over raw mushrooms will help retain color, especially desirable when using uncooked in recipes or as crudités.

USAGE

These mushrooms are quite versatile and work well in most cooking methods. They are delicious marinated, skewered and grilled, sliced and served as crudités with dip, stir-fried, sautéed, incorporated into baked recipes, deep-fried, roasted, and broiled. The whole mushroom, from cap to stem, may be eaten, so there is no waste by the pound. Toss into recipes along with wild or exotic varieties to keep cost down and mushroom count up.

Ideal with meats and poultry, white mushrooms especially enhance grilled steaks and chicken breasts when sautéed with onion and garlic. You can also sauté sliced mushrooms and incorporate them into cream and tomato sauces.

Criminis *(Agaricus bisporus, A. brunnescens)*

Crimini mushrooms, also known as browns, Italian browns, baby portabellas, or baby bellas, are as adaptable in recipes as white mushrooms. They resemble their white cousins in size and shape but have a richer flavor and chocolate-colored caps. They are cultivated in composted beds like white mushrooms but have a crisper, denser texture because of a different strand of spore used to inoculate the growing medium. Crimini and white mushrooms may be used interchangeably.

White and crimini mushrooms ready for cooking.

PURCHASING

When selecting any mushroom, use common sense. Bruises and discoloration usually are a result of poor handling or storage. Dry, shriveled mushrooms reflect their age. As with white mushrooms, choose criminis that have firm, smooth caps with intact veils.

PUTTING AWAY

They will stay fresh for at least four to five days in the refrigerator. Clean, store, and use crimini mushrooms as you would white mushrooms.

Portabellas *(Agaricus bisporus)*

Portabella, sometimes spelled portobello, is the largest and most popular commercially grown variety of mushroom. It is directly related to both white and crimini mushrooms. Portabellas are cultivated in richly composted, tiered shelves, like the other two *Agaricus bisporus* mushroom varieties. They actually are crimini mushrooms that have been left to grow for up to a week longer, picked when the caps reach 3 to 6 inches. Because of their maturity at picking time, their dark, inky gills are always exposed. They also have a drier cap texture and deeper, meatier flavor than their crimini sisters. Portabellas are often referred to as "the filet mignon of mushrooms" because of their beefy texture and taste.

PURCHASING

Portabellas are sold in plastic-wrapped packages or loosely strewn in baskets and sold in bulk. Caps should be dry textured and firm, but not brittle and broken around the edges. Flattened-out caps suggest older mushrooms and stronger flavor. They are sold whole, by the cap, or sliced.

PUTTING AWAY

Store loosely in original breathable container (not a plastic bag) or in a paper bag. Cover with damp paper towels to prevent caps from drying out once original packaging is removed. They will keep up to ten days.

TO CLEAN

Cultivated mushrooms do not need much cleaning. Any little clumps of what resembles dirt are bits of growing medium such as peat. Wipe loosely attached dirt specks clean with damp paper towel. Trim stem

Portabella mushrooms, ready to pick.

even with cap. Some recipes call for inky, dark gills to be removed; if so, gently scrape out with a spoon and discard.

USAGE

Portabella mushrooms hold up well next to strong, meaty flavors. Their soul mates are grilled steaks and chops, but they also go well with game and chicken. Substitute portabellas for meat to make delicious vegetarian dishes. Caps or thick slices are superstars of the grill, with a buttery, beef tenderloin–like texture.

Portabella caps may be stuffed with almost anything, from crabmeat to vegetables to strips of meat and cheese. Caps may be broiled, roasted, or sliced and sautéed. Portabellas are extremely versatile, adding texture and steaklike flavor to stir-fries, soups, appetizers, pasta, and grilled and baked entrées.

For a quick appetizer, arrange spinach, crisp bacon, and Gorgonzola cheese over caps at the end of grilling or broiling, and splash with balsamic vinaigrette. Broil stuffed caps just until spinach wilts and cheese softens. Serve hot.

Shiitakes (*Lentinus edodes*)

Shiitakes are one of the most commonly cultivated or harvested mushrooms in the world. Also known as oak, Chinese, or black forest mushrooms, they are characterized by tan to brown, open umbrella-shaped caps; fibrous, cream-colored stems; and milky white exposed gills. Caps range in size from 1 to 3 inches. These mushrooms grow on oak logs in forests or commercially on man-made stumps of oak sawdust, wheat bran, and millet grain in growing houses. They are widely available both fresh and dried.

PURCHASING

Caps should be firm and smooth, not brittle. They curl slightly inward around the edges. Condensation sometimes builds up inside plastic-wrapped packages, so check to make sure caps don't look wet, water-damaged, or broken. Alternatively, buy them loosely sold in bulk and place in paper bags.

PUTTING AWAY

Store shiitakes in the refrigerator, either in a paper bag or other breathable container. They can last up to two weeks.

TO CLEAN

If cleaning is necessary, dab caps with moist paper towels. Trim off the woody, fibrous stems, and discard or reserve to flavor soups and stocks.

USAGE

The firm, fleshy caps hold up well when grilled. Brush or spray caps with olive oil, and set directly on the grill rack. Shiitakes enhance risottos, pastas, stir-fries, fondues, egg dishes, casseroles, and grilled entrées with their distinctive chewy texture and intense woodsy flavor.

Maitakes *(Grifola frondosa)*

Maitakes are also referred to as hen of the woods, because in the wild this multiruffled fungus resembles a plump, meaty hen, and dancing mushrooms, because Japanese folklore depicts people dancing for joy when they found these mushrooms. Tiered mushroom "leaves" or fronds grow upward from a central whitish stem and can grow as large as a turkey, weighing 20 to 30 pounds. Grown much like shiitakes, along man-made logs in humidity-controlled rooms, these mushrooms resemble coral reefs. They are commercially grown year-round and also foraged in moist forests, showing up fresh at farmers' markets in summer and fall. Color ranges from beige to mousy brown. Their intense nutty flavor and chewy texture goes a long way in recipes.

PURCHASING

Choose firm, fresh-smelling clumps of mushrooms. They shouldn't be brittle around the leafy edges or look overly handled or damaged. Maitakes are not as omnipresent as portabellas or shiitakes but are showing up in supermarkets with more and more frequency, fetching up to $13 per pound.

PUTTING AWAY

Store loosely in a paper bag or other breathable container. This mushroom will keep up to a week in the refrigerator.

TO CLEAN

Wash under cold running water, if necessary.

USAGE

Maitakes are my favorite variety of mushroom. Their pronounced rich, nutty flavor is especially compatible with grilled meats and potato dishes. They have a unique chewiness and hold up well when braised, sautéed, or stewed.

Oyster mushrooms *(Pleurotus ostreatus)*, yellow oyster mushrooms *(Pleurotus citrinopileatus)*, or dark brown oyster mushrooms *(Pleurotus pulmonarius)*

Characterized by their fluted, fan-shaped caps and subtle oyster flavor, these multipurpose mushrooms come in a range of colors. Yellow, gray, and light brown are the most prominent shades, all having ivory-colored gills and long, white stems. Oyster mushrooms vary in size from 3 to 5 inches.

PURCHASING

Oyster mushrooms are packaged and widely available year-round in supermarkets. Look for containers that are not dripping with condensation. Caps should be silky smooth and velvety looking, not droopy or overly handled.

PUTTING AWAY

Store loosely in original breathable container, a paper bag, or an air-vented container covered lightly with a damp paper towel in refrigerator. They will keep up to a week if refrigerated.

TO CLEAN

These mushrooms hardly need to be cleaned. You may want to dab or dislodge any specks caught in wider-spaced gills gently with a paper towel, but that's it. Trim off the very ends of the stems.

USAGE

The silky texture of these velvety mushrooms highlights soups, sauces, and side dishes. With its slippery sautéed consistency, subtle shellfish flavor, and faint shellfish scent, these mushrooms are reminiscent of fresh oysters and go well with veal, chicken, and especially seafood.

Royal trumpets *(Pleurotus eryngii)*

Royal trumpet mushroom caps look like dimpled cheeks. They range in color from beige to tan to light brown and have long, white stems, which are edible too. Royal trumpet mushrooms are available across the United States. These tender, long-stemmed mushrooms are very delicate, and you can eat the whole thing.

PURCHASING

Look for intact caps and dry packaging. Moisture will form splotches on caps and break down their silky exterior.

PUTTING AWAY

Store in a paper bag or breathable container covered with a damp paper towel in the lower portion of the refrigerator. Will keep for three to four days.

TO CLEAN

Royal trumpets probably don't need much washing. Any dark specks may be shaken out or picked clean using a moist paper towel. Don't clean until right before using so as not to disturb the delicate surface. If needed, trim off the very ends of the stems.

USAGE

Royal trumpet mushrooms have a faint scallop-oyster flavor and pair well with seafood. The stems and caps can give a subtle seafood flavor to cream sauces and soups. The trumpet-shaped caps, when sautéed, have a limp, moist texture.

Enokis *(Flammulina velutipes)*

These tiny, white mushrooms have caps that resemble pearls suspended on thin white stems. They are also known as snow or winter mushrooms, because they are foraged in the wild from fall through early winter. Some caps are grown a little bigger in size and resemble miniature white parasols with ruffled edges. Enokis are commercially grown and are available year-round.

PURCHASING

Look for plastic packaging, with intact, slender, delicate stalks and caps. They should look crisp, fresh, and uniformly white.

PUTTING AWAY

Unopened packages of enoki mushrooms will keep up to a week and a half in the refrigerator. Once unsealed, use up the mushrooms in the next day or two.

TO CLEAN

Grown straight up out of sterilized plastic bottles and then trimmed off, enoki mushrooms are clean and don't require any washing. Just before using, simply trim off the lower third of the slender stems, and carefully pull the mushrooms apart into small clusters.

USAGE

Enoki mushrooms, caps and stems, may be eaten fresh or lightly sautéed. Lightly toss fresh mushrooms into salads, or sauté quickly and incorporate into stir-fries. Fresh, crisp-tender enokis can make whimsical garnishes laid across fish entrées or floating delicately atop soups or sauces.

Beech mushrooms *(Hypsizygus tessulatus)*

Beech mushrooms are vastly popular in Japan, where they are also known as hon-shimeji mushrooms. In northern North America, they are foraged in the wild from high atop hardwood trees between September and December. They are also cultivated year-round in plastic bottles in the same fashion as enokis. Their smooth caps range from milky white to light yellow, tan to light brown.

PURCHASING

Clumps of beech mushrooms should look perky and crisp; don't buy them if they look shriveled and dry like parched sun-bathers. They tend to be more expensive than other specialty mushrooms.

PUTTING AWAY

Store in a colander loosely covered with barely damp paper towels on the lower shelf of the refrigerator. Before washing, store in a paper bag in the refrigerator.

TO CLEAN

Because of the way they are grown, cultivated beech mushrooms do not require cleaning. If foraged, or if you do desire to clean them, rinse them in a colander under cold running water and let dry on a tea towel. Trim off the very bottom portion of the central stem.

USAGE

Beech mushrooms may be used as a nutty, crisp-tender addition to stuffings, stir-fries, pastas and stews, or as a garnish. Use caps delicately sautéed and strewn atop soups or sauces.

Pom pom mushrooms *(Hericium erinaceus)*

These soft, feathery mushrooms look like tiny white pom poms—picture-perfect balls that are all frills and no stem.

PURCHASING

Pom pom mushrooms should be pearly white all over, without any signs of yellowish aging or brown splotches. They smell bad when they have been lingering on shelves too long. Sometimes the smell is not noticeable until you have peeled away the packaging, and by then the mushrooms are sitting on your kitchen counter.

PUTTING AWAY

Store mushrooms loosely in a paper bag or in a breathable container covered loosely with a paper towel or tea towel. Place in the lower portion of the refrigerator. They will keep two to three days.

TO CLEAN

These mushrooms don't require any cleaning or trimming.

Pom pom mushrooms are light and airy in texture. Their long, feathery wisps absorb and take up the flavor of whatever's poured into the pan. They taste best lightly sautéed in butter with shallots and a little wine or stock. They also are delicious sliced or whole and mixed in with, or as a vegetarian substitute for, seafood, veal, or chicken.

Wild Mushrooms

Three prominent wild mushrooms are often found fresh or dried at farmers' markets and are also cropping up in gourmet food stores: morels, porcinis, and chanterelles.

MORELS (*Morchella* spp.)

The growing season for morels begins in frost-free spring and continues until about the end of July. During this time, they may be available in the produce section of grocery stores or at farmers' markets selling for $17 to $29 a pound. Their gumdrop-shaped, honeycombed caps easily identify these foraged or cultivated mushrooms. These deeply furrowed caps require a lot of cleaning to dislodge dirt and sand. Blanching them in a pot of boiling water, then refreshing under cold running water, softens their firm texture and dislodges dirt particles and insects. Some of their intense flavor is sacrificed when blanching, however. Briefly soaking in a bowl of salted water will also dislodge dirt from the caps. Cut off the stems before cooking and slice larger caps in half.

The distinctive rich, soil-scented flavor of morels is brought out best by sautéing them gently in butter with a splash of calvados or white wine and adding heavy cream. They also make crisp-tender earthy bites when stirred into egg dishes and cream-laced sauces.

PORCINIS (*Boletus edulis*)

Porcini mushrooms are aptly named—*porcini* means "little piglet" in Italian. Comical looking stems resemble bulging pork bellies. They are also known as *cepes,* the French name, *steinpilz* in German, or *bolete* in English. Porcinis have pale yellowish brown to dark reddish brown rounded caps atop bulbous ivory stems. They grow anywhere from 2 to over 8 inches. Porcinis are gathered in the wild and imported mainly from Italy and France for several weeks in summer to late fall. They are also grown commercially in pockets of the United States, surfacing at farmers' markets and at specialty food stores. The rich, earth-scented flavor and meaty texture of these mushrooms make them ideal grilling candidates.

Dried or flash-frozen are more readily available than perishable fresh porcinis, although texture (leathery when reconstituted) and flavor are somewhat sacrificed. Look for packages of whole mushroom pieces, not dusty bits. They should be free of mold, mildew, and pinholes, where little worms have crawled in. Dried porcinis have an intense woodsy flavor that in minimal handfuls permeates soups, sauces, risotto, and pasta dishes. Dried pieces require constituting in warm liquid like water, stock, or wine before using.

CHANTERELLES *(Cantharellus cibarius)*

Chanterelles crop up from around July until January. These sought-after foraged mushrooms have a distinctive apricot color and sweet perfume. To clean, wipe with damp paper towel and remove stems. Incorporate caps in cream-based or light brothy sauces. The subtle fruit flavor of chanterelles blends well with grilled seafood, chops, risotto, and pasta dishes.

Truffles

Truffles are used to add an exquisite aromatic flavor to many dishes. Chefs slip them gently under poultry skins, fold them carefully into eggs, or stir them into silky sauces.

Foraged from mid-November to March, and mainly coming from the Perigord region of France and northern Italy, winter black truffles *(Tuber melanosporum)* are available fresh around the holidays at specialty stores and markets. They can be purchased year-round either flash-frozen or in jars. They are distinguished from summer truffles by their jet-black interiors and whitish streaks. Unlike white truffles, black truffles do not lose their flavor when cooked. Black truffles impart a wonderful, distinctive, musty-earth flavor to roasted chicken, brunch-layered egg dishes, scalloped potatoes, meat-laced pastas, paté, and cream-based sauces.

Equally satisfying are the white truffles *(Tuber magnatum)*, found mainly in the northern Alba region of Italy. The scent of these buried treasures is so strong, it permeates up to 16 inches of surrounding earth. Specially trained dogs and female pigs are a must in finding the underground fruiting bodies. White truffles have an irregular, somewhat bumpy, circular shape and light brownish exterior. The pale brown interior is characterized by white veins. They are best finely diced and strewn raw over eggs, sautééd potatoes, or creamy risotto dishes. Also gaining in popularity is the Oregon white truffle. White truffles range in size from as small as a quarter to as large as a woman's fist and weigh between 1 and 4 ounces. Best eaten fresh when available in the winter months, they are also sold year-round flash-frozen. They need to be washed and scrubbed free of dirt before cooking. They may be kept refrigerated for up to ten days, but their flavor fades so they are best eaten very fresh.

Summer truffles *(Tuber aestivum)*, found in the spring and summer months in pockets of Europe and Asia, are similar in appearance to winter truffles with their bumpy brownish black surface, but have murky white centers. They are considerably less expensive than winter black or white truffles, as their flavor is noticeably inferior and less pungent. You get what you pay for in this case.

Occasionally, local supermarkets will carry truffles around the winter holidays. I noticed black blobs tucked in plastic wrap on a shelf next to cuts of beef in December. The butcher behind the counter wasn't sure where they were from, so I opted for a handful of fresh shiitakes from the produce section. Not the same flavor, but much cheaper.

Dried Mushrooms

Dried mushrooms augment the flavor of soups, sauces, and stews. If the fresh version of a mushroom variety is hard to find or nonexistent in your area, dried mushrooms make a good substitute. When selecting dried mushrooms, make sure they haven't been on the shelf or hook for too long or appear infiltrated by insects. Mushroom pieces should be intact, not in small broken bits.

Buy ample packets. After soaking and reconstituting, you may find you're a handful short. They plump up to double or even triple their dried size, but even so, I always seem to need more than what's bobbing in the soaking liquid.

When you get them home, transfer them to Ziploc bags and store them in the freezer or cupboard. Dried mushrooms will last longer this way.

When ready to use, reconstitute dried mushrooms for 20 to 30 minutes in a hot liquid such as stock, water, or wine. Squish them around with your fingertips to see if they are completely softened. Carefully remove the rehydrated mushrooms, then strain the soaking liquid through coffee filters or double layers of cheesecloth. Use the liquid immediately or freeze in ice cube trays, then place in Ziploc bags to flavor cooking liquids at a later date. Alternatively, you can simply discard the soaking liquid.

Appetizers and Starters

One of the messiest finger foods, stuffed mushrooms are the most prolific and omnipresent appetizers on the cocktail tray, from those with basic breadcrumb stuffing to fancier creations with lump crabmeat or ham and Swiss fillings. The new crop of exotic mushrooms opens up new mushroom caps to fill. I've included a drippingly delicious Alsatian Stuffed Portabella Caps recipe that demands to stay on the plate. Use a fork and knife with these oversize caps, or you'll wear them down your front for the rest of the evening. The other recipes in this chapter are equally mouth-watering, so don't plan your next party without some starters from this lineup.

Different varieties of mushrooms add exotic flavors to food.

Alsatian Stuffed Portabella Caps

Offset the richness of these lusciously filled mushroom caps by serving atop lightly dressed greens interspersed with wisps of radicchio.

2 tablespoons balsamic vinegar

3 tablespoons olive oil

I garlic clove, minced

4 portabella mushroom caps, wiped clean

6 slices hickory-smoked bacon

2 tablespoons butter

I large sweet onion, chopped (about 2 cups)

I roasted red pepper (page 102), cut into small dices

I medium tomato, diced

$^1/_2$ teaspoon salt

$^1/_4$ teaspoon freshly ground black pepper

$^3/_4$ cup shredded Danish fontina cheese, about 3 ounces

2 tablespoons chopped flat-leaf parsley

Preheat broiler and position rack on top shelf. Line a cookie sheet with foil. Spray or oil foil.

In small bowl, whisk together vinegar, olive oil, and garlic. Brush both sides of mushroom caps with marinade, and set on prepared cookie sheet. Broil until darkened, about 2 minutes on each side. Set aside. Reduce oven to 425 degrees.

In large, heavy skillet over moderate heat, cook bacon until crisp. Drain on paper towels, crumble, and set aside. Pour off fat from pan.

Add butter to skillet. Over moderate heat, sauté onion, stirring occasionally until softened and golden, about 20 minutes. Stir in red pepper and tomato, and cook 2 minutes longer. Season vegetables with salt and pepper, and remove from heat. Stir in cheese and parsley.

Top broiled mushroom caps with vegetable mixture. Sprinkle with crumbled bacon. Bake caps in 425-degree oven until reheated throughout, about 8 minutes. Serve warm. Makes 4 servings.

Time-saving shortcuts

Substitute roasted peppers purchased in jars at the supermarket or gourmet food shops. Drain on paper towels to soak up excess liquid.

Substitute balsamic vinaigrette or Italian dressing for vinegar, olive oil, and garlic marinade.

Substitute preshredded mozzarella and Parmesan cheese for fontina. Danish fontina is superior, however, with its slightly nutty flavor and creamy texture that melts on the tongue.

Mushroom Polenta Squares

This versatile recipe may be served at room temperature or chilled and cut into bitesize pieces as an appetizer, or hot from the oven as a side dish.

1 recipe Polenta (page 95)

2 tablespoons butter

1 pound mixed mushrooms, such as crimini, oyster, shiitake, or button, sliced

8 ounces cream cheese

1 egg

1 garlic clove, minced

¹/₂ teaspoon salt

pinch red pepper flakes

¹/₂ cup thinly sliced green onions

³/₄ cup grated cheddar cheese

Preheat oven to 400 degrees. Prepare polenta. In large skillet over moderate heat, melt butter. Add mushrooms and cook until liquid evaporates and mushrooms are softened, about 5 minutes. Set aside to cool slightly.

In food processor, blend cream cheese, egg, garlic, salt, and red pepper flakes until smooth. Spread mixture over polenta. Sprinkle mushrooms evenly over top, then sprinkle green onions and cheddar cheese over mushrooms. Bake for 15 minutes, until cheddar cheese is melted and cream cheese layer is set. Makes 8 servings.

Time-saving shortcut

Buy rolls of polenta, available in the produce section of your local supermarket.

Roasted Pear and Gorgonzola Soufflé with Shiitake Pear Chutney

This soufflé will provoke a hush as it's brought to the table. The subtle sweetness of the pear puree and Gorgonzola cheese pair well with the chunky mushroom chutney.

- 6 tablespoons unsalted butter, divided
- 4 firm, ripe pears (1 1/2 pounds), such as Bosc or Bartlett, sliced 1/4 inch thick (about 4 cups)
- 1 tablespoon sugar
- 4 tablespoons flour
- 1 1/2 cups warm milk
- 6 eggs, separated
- 1/4 pound Gorgonzola cheese, crumbled (about 1 1/4 cups)
- 1/2 teaspoon freshly chopped or 1/4 teaspoon dried sage
- 1/4 teaspoon salt
- 1/8 teaspoon freshly ground pepper

Preheat oven to 400 degrees. Butter an 8-cup soufflé dish. In large skillet over medium-high heat, melt 2 tablespoons butter. Add pear slices and sauté until softened, about 3 minutes. Sprinkle sugar over pears and continue to sauté until golden and translucent, about 5 more minutes.

In a food processor, puree 3/4 cup of the cooked pears until smooth. Set aside. Coarsely chop remaining pear slices and set aside to be used in chutney.

In large saucepan over medium heat, melt remaining 4 tablespoons butter. Whisk in flour and cook roux until white and frothy, 3 to 5 minutes. Whisk in warm milk and boil 1 minute. Stir in egg yolks and pear puree. Remove from heat. Stir in crumbled cheese, sage, salt, and pepper. Mixture will be slightly lumpy.

In large bowl, beat egg whites just until stiff peaks form. Fold into warm cheese mixture. Scrape into prepared soufflé dish and place in preheated oven.

While soufflé is baking, prepare chutney. Bake soufflé for 30 minutes, until crown is golden and cracks begin to brown. Serve immediately with Shiitake Pear Chutney on the side. Makes 6 servings.

SHIITAKE PEAR CHUTNEY

3 tablespoons olive oil

2 medium shallots, minced (about $1/3$ cup)

I garlic clove, minced

3 $1/2$ ounces shiitakes, stems removed, thinly sliced (about 1 $1/2$ cups loosely packed)

I tablespoon balsamic vinegar

I teaspoon chopped fresh parsley

I cup coarsely chopped sautéed pear slices

salt and pepper to taste

In large saucepan over moderately high heat, heat olive oil. Stir in shallots and garlic, and cook 1 minute. Add shiitake mushrooms and sauté until tender, about 3 minutes. Remove from heat. Stir in vinegar and parsley. Gently stir in reserved coarsely chopped pears. Season with salt and pepper to taste. Scrape into serving dish to pass with soufflé. Chutney can be prepared a day in advance and rewarmed in the microwave.

Mushroom Pâté Phyllo Cups

Basic mushroom filling, or duxelles, as it's called in France, is a mixture of sautéed shallots and mushrooms. The mixture is used in this recipe to fill prebaked phyllo dough shells.

I recipe Duxelles (page 92)

I package (15) frozen mini phyllo dough shells

chopped parsley or cilantro for garnish

Prepare mushroom filling (duxelles). Keep warm. Heat phyllo shells according to package directions. Fill each baked shell with 1 rounded tablespoon of mushroom filling. Garnish with chopped parsley or cilantro and serve warm. Make 15 shells.

Time-saving shortcut

Make the duxelles up to 2 days in advance and refrigerate. Reheat filling in microwave before using.

Smoky Shiitake Tomato Toasts

This recipe may be made a day or two ahead of time. Keep toasts in an airtight container and refrigerate tomato mixture. Assemble and sprinkle with cheese and broil when ready to serve.

> 12 half-inch slices of French bread (baguette)
> 5 tablespoons olive oil
> 1 teaspoon garlic salt or 1 garlic clove, halved
> 2 cups sliced shiitake mushrooms
> 1 medium tomato, peeled, seeded, and finely diced
>   (about $1/_2$ cup)
> 1 teaspoon mushroom soy sauce (page 102)
>   or dark soy sauce
> 1 tablespoon chopped fresh chives, basil, or parsley
> salt and pepper to taste
> $1/_3$ cup shredded smoked Gouda or fontina cheese

Preheat oven to 375 degrees. Place bread slices on a baking sheet. Brush each side with 3 tablespoons of the olive oil. Sprinkle tops of slices with garlic salt or rub with fresh garlic. Bake, flipping once, until golden brown, 10 to 15 minutes. Remove and turn oven to broil.

In medium skillet over moderate heat, heat remaining 2 tablespoons olive oil. Add mushrooms and cook until lightly softened, 3 to 5 minutes. Stir in tomato and soy sauce, and cook 1 minute longer. Stir in chopped herb. Season with salt and pepper to taste. Mound mixture on toasts and sprinkle with cheese. Broil until cheese begins to melt, about 1 minute. Serve warm or at room temperature. Makes 12 toasts.

Time-saving shortcut

Substitute crostini for baguette slices.

Mediterranean Mushroom
Bruschetta

Ficelle is French for "string" or "stick" and is the name of the skinny, smaller loaves of French bread used in this recipe.

**small French bread loaf (ficelle), cut diagonally
into 12 slices**

3 garlic cloves, peeled

$1/4$ cup plus 3 tablespoons olive oil

1 small onion, chopped (about $1/2$ cup)

**6 ounces portabella caps, gills scraped out,
chopped**

1 red bell pepper, chopped

2 tablespoons balsamic vinegar

$1/2$ teaspoon salt

3 tablespoons freshly chopped basil leaves

$1/8$ teaspoon freshly ground black pepper

pinch crushed red pepper flakes

$1/4$ cup crumbled feta cheese, about $1 1/2$ ounces

Preheat oven to 400 degrees. Cut one garlic clove in half and rub on ficelle slices. Place slices on cookie sheet and brush with $1/4$ cup of the olive oil. Bake 12 minutes, flipping once, until golden on both sides. Set aside.

In heavy skillet over moderate heat, heat the remaining 3 tablespoons of olive oil. Mince remaining 2 garlic cloves and sauté with onion until softened, about 5 minutes. Stir in mushrooms and sauté until tender, about 4 minutes. Stir in red bell pepper and vinegar, and cook 1 minute longer. Stir in seasonings, then fold in feta cheese. Dollop about 1 tablespoon mixture on each slice of garlic toast. Makes 12 bruschetta.

Mushroom
Brie en Croute

There's no need to serve crackers with this stunning crust-wrapped, mushroom-scented Brie cheese. Green and purple grapes and twisted orange slices add wonderful splashes of color around the perimeter of the serving platter.

2 tablespoons unsalted butter

3 ounces wild mushrooms (such as shiitake, oyster, crimini), finely chopped

2 green onions, chopped

$1/4$ teaspoon fresh or $1/8$ teaspoon dried thyme

salt and pepper

1 sheet frozen puff pastry, thawed

1 egg, beaten

4-pound Brie wheel

Preheat oven to 375 degrees. In small skillet, melt butter. Sauté mushrooms and onions until soft, 3 to 5 minutes. Season with thyme, salt, and pepper. Let cool.

Roll out puff pastry on lightly floured surface to about $1/8$-inch thickness. Cut out a 10-inch circle. Brush circle with egg, and spread cooled mushroom mixture in center of circle. Set Brie wheel over top of mushroom mixture. Brush top and sides of wheel with egg. Carefully fold pastry around edges and over top of Brie. Be sure to enclose cheese wheel completely with pastry, or cheese will leak out in the oven.

Gently flip pastry-wrapped cheese, seam side down, on lightly greased baking sheet. Brush all over with egg. If desired, decorate top with pastry trimmings and brush with egg. Bake for 25 to 30 minutes, or until golden brown and puffed.

Marinated Mushroom and Roasted Red Pepper Antipasto

These marinated mushrooms can be made 3 or 4 days in advance and stored in the refrigerator. When ready to serve, strain marinating liquid and reserve for use in pastas or salads. Skewered on toothpicks, these mushrooms and red peppers make a lovely accompaniment to an appetizer tray of assorted cheeses and salami. The white balsamic vinegar provides a fruity, bold flavor, but white wine vinegar will work too.

$1/2$ cup white balsamic or white wine vinegar

I cup water

$3/4$ teaspoon salt

I pound crimini or button mushrooms, washed and trimmed (slice or quarter large ones)

2 garlic cloves, thinly sliced

I teaspoon dried oregano

I teaspoon dried marjoram

I roasted red pepper (page 102), cut into $1/2$-inch strips

$1/2$ cup extra-virgin olive oil

In large saucepan, bring vinegar, water, and salt to a boil. Stir in mushrooms, cover, and simmer for 6 minutes, until tender. Remove from heat and stir in remaining ingredients. Place warm mixture in decorative glass or ceramic bowl, and pass with crusty bread slices. Makes 4 to 6 servings.

Alternatively, strain liquid, spear mushroom and red pepper strips on toothpicks, and serve cold or at room temperature on an appetizer tray.

Time-saving shortcut

Use store-bought jars or deli-made roasted red peppers instead of roasting peppers yourself.

Mushroom Pastry Straws

2 tablespoons butter

2 shallots, minced

$1/2$ pound crimini or button mushrooms, cleaned and finely chopped

2 tablespoons chopped parsley

2 teaspoons lemon juice

$1/4$ teaspoon salt

$1/8$ teaspoon freshly ground pepper

17.3-ounce package frozen pastry sheets (2 sheets), thawed

1 egg

1 tablespoon water

$1/2$ cup grated Gruyère or Swiss cheese (about 2 ounces)

Preheat oven to 400 degrees. In large skillet over moderately high heat, melt butter. Add shallots and cook, stirring, until softened, about 2 minutes. Stir in mushrooms and cook until excess liquid is evaporated, about 6 minutes. Stir in parsley, lemon juice, and seasonings; cook 1 minute longer. Let cool. Set aside.

On lightly floured work surface, roll out pastry sheets to form 10-by-12-inch rectangles. In small bowl, combine egg and water. Brush each pastry sheet with egg wash. Spread mushroom mixture over one egg-washed sheet. Sprinkle with cheese. Flip other pastry sheet, egg-wash side down, over mushroom mixture. Press down lightly over top sheet.

Cut filled pastry sheets in half lengthwise. Cut each half into 20 half-inch-wide "straws." Carefully twist straws, and space evenly apart on ungreased cookie sheet. Bake for 10 minutes, or until pastry is golden. Cool on wire racks. Serve at room temperature. Makes 40 straws.

Spicy Battered Mushrooms
with Ranch Dipping Sauce

These fried, batter-dipped mushrooms are made with a deliciously light, somewhat zippy batter. Sweet onion rings and sliced zucchini taste great made with this batter too.

- 1 cup flour
- $1/2$ teaspoon baking soda
- 1 teaspoon fajita seasoning, Southwestern seasoning, or Old Bay seasoning
- $1/2$ teaspoon salt
- $1/8$ teaspoon freshly ground black pepper
- 1 egg
- 1 cup buttermilk
- 4 cups vegetable oil
- 10 ounces crimini, shiitake, or oyster mushrooms, stems removed, caps brushed clean

In small bowl, combine flour, baking soda, and seasonings. In another small bowl, use a fork to stir together egg and buttermilk. Stir buttermilk mixture into flour mixture until just combined.

In 2-quart saucepan, heat oil to about 350 degrees, or just until small bubbles form around bits of batter when dropped into hot oil. Using two forks, dip mushroom caps in batter to cover. Gently fork mushrooms into hot oil. Fry mushrooms 2 or 3 to a batch, until deep golden brown. Remove to serving platter and serve immediately. Pass with Ranch Dipping Sauce. Serves 4 to 6.

RANCH DIPPING SAUCE

- $1/2$ cup mayonnaise
- $1/4$ cup plus 2 tablespoons buttermilk
- $1/2$ teaspoon fajita seasoning, Southwestern seasoning, or Old Bay seasoning
- $1/4$ teaspoon garlic salt
- pinch crushed red pepper flakes or cayenne pepper

Stir together all ingredients in small bowl and pass along with battered mushrooms.

Steamed Asian Veal Dumplings with Porcini Soy Dipping Sauce

These dumplings are moist and juicy—pass them with plenty of napkins. The subtle veal flavor is enhanced by the unique rustic flavor of porcini mushroom bits, a delicious combination. If you can't find porcinis, you can substitute shiitake mushrooms.

$1/_3$ cup dried porcini mushrooms
I pound ground veal
$1/_2$ cup plus 2 tablespoons hot water
I egg white
$1/_2$ cup scallions, finely chopped
I tablespoon grated fresh ginger
I tablespoon soy sauce
I tablespoon sesame oil
I teaspoon grated lemon zest
$1/_2$ teaspoon salt
$1/_2$ teaspoon hot chili oil
$1/_8$ teaspoon pepper
I 2-ounce package wonton wrappers
bok choy leaves, optional

Soak mushrooms in hot water for 20 minutes. Strain mushroom pieces and finely chop. Reserve soaking liquid to use in dipping sauce.

In large bowl, using clean hands or a fork, mix together all ingredients except the wonton wrappers until just combined. Spoon 1 rounded teaspoon of veal filling into the center of each wrapper. Moisten edges of wrappers with water. Bring opposite corners of the wrappers to the center, and using forefinger and thumb, pinch together over top the veal. Bring remaining points to the center and pinch the side seams closed to form a dumpling. Alternatively, fold wrappers in half on the diagonal and press edges together to form triangles.

Set dumplings spaciously apart in the top of a steamer. (You can steam them in the steamer portion of a rice cooker.) Cover and steam for 4 to 5 minutes, or until no longer pink inside. Serve dumplings on a platter lined with bok choy leaves, and pass with Porcini Soy Dipping Sauce. Makes 35 to 40 dumplings.

PORCINI SOY DIPPING SAUCE

  3 tablespoons soy sauce
  3 tablespoons porcini mushroom soaking liquid
  I tablespoon sesame oil
  I tablespoon lemon juice
  I sliver fresh garlic
  I teaspoon minced green onions
  pinch crushed red pepper flakes or few drops hot chili oil

In small bowl, combine all ingredients. Serve alongside dumplings. This recipe may be easily doubled. Makes about $\frac{1}{2}$ cup.

Crab-Stuffed Mushrooms

Fresh local crabmeat from cracked northwestern Dungeness crabs makes these stuffed caps even more sweetly flavorful.

  14 large white stuffer mushrooms, stems removed
  3 tablespoons melted butter, divided
  2 tablespoons mayonnaise
  I tablespoon lemon juice
  I teaspoon Worcestershire sauce
  I tablespoon chopped flat-leaf Italian parsley
  I tablespoon snipped fresh chives
  $\frac{1}{2}$ teaspoon garlic powder
  I scant teaspoon Old Bay seasoning
  pinch cayenne
  $\frac{1}{2}$ cup crushed thin whole-wheat crackers, such as Breton (about 8)
  8 ounces crabmeat

Preheat oven to 350 degrees. Place mushrooms in a shallow glass pan, such as a 10-inch pie pan. Coat mushrooms all over with 2 table-spoons of the melted butter, using a pastry brush or by dipping.

In medium bowl, stir together mayonnaise, lemon juice, Worces-tershire, herbs and spices, and crushed crackers until well combined. Fold in crabmeat.

Using a tablespoon measure, mound crab mixture into each mush-room cap. Drizzle crab-stuffed mushrooms with remaining table-spoon of melted butter. Bake in oven until heated through, about 10 minutes. Serve hot. Makes 14 stuffed caps.

Mushrooms augment the flavor and texture of any soup.

Soups

Soups are a wonderful way to use up extra mushrooms. If I have a surplus of mushrooms, I store them in my freezer in an ongoing Ziploc bag labeled, "sautéed mushrooms." (See Frozen Mushrooms on page 103.) In another plastic bag, I store stems and pieces of mushrooms that aren't conducive to eating, such as fibrous shiitake stems or central stem ends trimmed from maitake mushrooms. These mushroom bits can be simmered in stocks and sauces to extract their earthy flavor, then strained for a lovely mushroom-scented broth. I've included a recipe in this section specifically for using up either fresh or frozen mushrooms: Mushroom Consommé with Garlic-Sage Croutons, an aromatic broth that just might give chicken noodle soup some competition as a cold remedy.

Mushrooms pair well with a myriad of vegetables, meats, seafoods, and grains. They heighten the flavor and texture of most soups and thickened potages. A handful of mushrooms can add a rich depth of flavor to a basic potato soup recipe, as in the Velvety Potato Mushroom Potage. Give water- or broth-based soups added richness by floating pads of Mushroom Butter (page 103) or drizzling Truffle-Scented Oil (page 103) over the surface just before serving.

This chapter includes a variety of different-textured soups, from the hearty Roasted Garlic, Mushroom, and Leek Bisque to the light and lively Mushroom Vegetable Soup. Crimini, portabella, white, shiitake, maitake, morel, trumpet, and oyster mushrooms hold up well in simmered heartier soups and stews. Light, feathery enoki and beech mushrooms are best added to soups at the last minute as a garnish.

Most of the recipes call for chicken stock or beef broth. You can make these yourself, following the recipes on pages 96 and 97, or you can substitute canned broth as a time-saving shortcut.

Mushroom Vegetable Soup

This soup is quick and easy to prepare. You can make it a day in advance and reheat in the microwave just before serving.

2 strips bacon

I tablespoon extra-virgin olive oil

I small onion, chopped (about $\frac{1}{2}$ cup)

2 carrots, peeled and diced

2 cups sliced white, oyster, crimini, maitake, or beech mushrooms

I teaspoon fresh or $\frac{1}{2}$ teaspoon dried thyme

I garlic clove, minced

$\frac{1}{4}$ teaspoon freshly ground black pepper

I $\frac{2}{3}$ cups Chicken Stock (page 96)

I $\frac{1}{2}$ cup water

6 fresh plum tomatoes, peeled and seeded

$\frac{2}{3}$ cup tomato juice

6 tablespoons Parmesan cheese

In large saucepan over moderate heat, cook bacon until crisp, about 3 minutes. Drain on paper towels, crumble, and reserve. Pour off any excess bacon grease from pan.

Add olive oil to the same pan, and over moderate heat, cook onions, carrots, and mushrooms until softened, about 6 minutes. Stir in thyme, garlic, and pepper, and cook 1 minute longer. Stir in chicken broth, water, tomatoes, and tomato juice. Bring to a boil, then reduce heat and simmer for 10 minutes. Ladle into bowls. Sprinkle with bacon and Parmesan cheese. Makes 6 servings.

Time-saving shortcut

Substitute a $14\frac{1}{2}$-ounce can of whole, peeled tomatoes in tomato juice for fresh tomatoes and tomato juice.

Butternut Squash Soup
with Oyster Mushrooms

For a richer, nuttier topping, use coarsely chopped maitake (hen of the woods) or shiitake mushroom caps in place of the milder oyster mushrooms.

5-pound butternut squash, halved lengthwise
3 tablespoons butter, divided
I medium onion, chopped
I carrot, chopped
2 garlic cloves, minced
$1/_4$ teaspoon pepper
$1/_4$ teaspoon nutmeg
$1/_4$ teaspoon salt
$3/_4$ cup white wine
$5 1/_4$ cups Chicken Stock (page 96)
2 cups coarsely chopped oyster mushroom caps
sour cream, for garnish
chopped fresh parsley, for garnish

Preheat oven to 350 degrees. Place squash on a baking sheet cut-side down, and bake 40 to 45 minutes, until flesh is tender when pricked with a fork. Scoop out seeds and discard. Scrape enough pulp from skin to make 4 cups and set aside.

In large saucepan over moderate heat, melt 2 tablespoons of the butter. Sauté onion, carrot, and garlic with seasonings until softened, about 8 minutes. Stir in wine and simmer until liquid is reduced by half. Stir in chicken stock and squash. Bring to a boil, then reduce heat and simmer for 5 minutes. Let cool slightly, and puree soup in batches in food processor or blender. Return to saucepan.

In small skillet over moderate heat, melt remaining 1 tablespoon of butter. Sauté mushrooms until tender and slightly browned, 6 to 8 minutes.

Spoon soup into bowls. Garnish with sour cream, rounded teaspoon of sautéed mushrooms, and sprinkle of chopped parsley. Makes 10 to 12 servings.

Roasted Garlic, Mushroom, and Leek Bisque

Woodsy and robust, this cold-weather soup is chock full of mushrooms and leeks. Roasted garlic adds faint sweetness to the creamy base. This substantial soup may be served as supper along with warmed rolls and crisp greens tossed with vinaigrette.

$3/4$ **pound portabella mushrooms (about four 4-inch caps or about 4$1/2$ cups sliced)**

$1/2$ **pound wild mushrooms, such as shiitake, maitake, trumpet, or oyster (about 4 cups loosely packed)**

I whole head garlic

$1/3$ **cup plus I teaspoon olive oil**

$1/2$ **teaspoon salt**

$1/8$ **teaspoon freshly ground pepper**

2 tablespoons unsalted butter

I large shallot, minced

I medium leek (dark green portion cut off), washed and chopped

3 cups Chicken Stock (page 96)

I cup heavy cream

sour cream for garnish

chopped chives for garnish

Preheat oven to 400 degrees. Remove stems from mushrooms, scrape dark gills from portabellas, and cut into $1/2$-inch pieces. Scatter over a cookie sheet lined with foil. Slice off tapered head of garlic just enough to expose tips of cloves. Place on a separate square of foil, large enough to enclose garlic head, and sprinkle with 1 teaspoon olive oil. Press foil together to enclose garlic. Sprinkle salt, pepper, and remaining $1/3$ cup of olive oil over mushrooms. Cover and seal mushrooms and garlic head with an additional sheet of foil. Roast them in the middle of the oven for 35 to 45 minutes, or until mushrooms and garlic buds are tender when pricked by knifepoint. (Some varieties of mushrooms may cook more quickly than the meatier portabellas. Check mushrooms after 30 minutes, and set aside any that appear softened and golden brown.)

Meanwhile, in large saucepan over moderate heat, melt butter and stir in shallot and leek. Cook, stirring, for 10 to 12 minutes, until vegetables are softened. Scrape mushrooms off of foil and add to leek and shallot. Squeeze garlic buds out of skins and add to mixture. Stir in chicken stock and bring to a boil. Remove from heat and allow to cool slightly. Working in 2 batches, puree mushroom mixture. Return pureed soup to saucepan and stir in cream; heat through. Adjust seasonings, then spoon into bowls. Garnish with sour cream and chopped fresh chives. Makes 6 to 8 servings.

Velvety Potato Mushroom Potage

Subtle potato flavor forms a silky curtain around earthy mushroom pieces. Sour cream and chives finish each serving with just the right amount of richness and flavor.

> 5 tablespoons butter, divided
>
> 1 medium onion, chopped
>
> 2 garlic cloves, minced
>
> 1 $^1/_2$ pounds baking potatoes (russet), coarsely chopped (about 4 cups)
>
> $^1/_2$ teaspoon dried marjoram, crumbled
>
> $^3/_4$ teaspoon salt
>
> 4 cups Chicken Stock (page 96)
>
> 4 ounces crimini, shiitake, or maitake mushrooms, coarsely chopped
>
> sour cream for garnish
>
> freshly snipped chives for garnish

In large saucepan, over moderate heat, melt 3 tablespoons of the butter. Sauté onion until softened, about 6 minutes. Stir in garlic, potatoes, marjoram, and salt. Cook 1 minute longer. Stir in chicken broth. Bring soup to a boil, then reduce to simmer. Cover and cook until potatoes are tender, 25 to 30 minutes.

Puree soup in batches until smooth in blender or food processor, and return to saucepan.

In small skillet, melt remaining 2 tablespoons butter, and cook mushrooms until softened, about 5 minutes. Stir mushrooms into soup and reheat. Ladle into bowls. Dollop with sour cream and sprinkle with chives. Makes 4 to 6 servings.

Porcini Mushroom Barley Soup

This stewlike mushroomy soup is hearty enough to serve as a light supper along with Mushroom Pastry Straws (page 30), homemade Parmesan Pepper Focaccia (page 94), or fresh buttered rolls. Dried shiitake mushrooms may be substituted for porcinis in this recipe.

$1/_2$ cup dried porcini mushroom pieces (about 1 ounce) or
   1 cup fresh, chopped porcinis and $1/_2$ cup chicken stock

$1/_2$ cup warm water

1 pound beef stew meat, trimmed and cut into 1-inch cubes

2 tablespoons flour

1 tablespoon paprika

$1/_2$ teaspoon salt

$1/_8$ teaspoon freshly ground black pepper

2 tablespoons olive oil

$1/_2$ cup red wine

2 tablespoons butter

3 garlic cloves, minced

1 medium onion, finely chopped

1 carrot, finely chopped

3 cups water, Chicken Stock (page 96), or Beef Broth
   (page 97)

1 bay leaf

1 teaspoon fresh or $1/_2$ teaspoon dried oregano

$14 1/_2$-ounce can stewed tomatoes with onion, celery, and peppers

$1/_4$ cup uncooked barley

In small bowl, soak mushrooms in warm water until reconstituted, about 20 minutes. Chop mushrooms, and strain and reserve soaking liquid.

Dredge beef cubes in flour seasoned with paprika, salt, and pepper. In large skillet over moderate heat, brown meat in oil on all sides for 6 to 8 minutes. Transfer to crockpot or large pot. Add red wine to skillet, scraping up any browned bits, and let reduce for 1 minute. Pour wine over meat.

In same skillet over moderate heat, melt butter. Stir in garlic, onion, and carrot, and cook until vegetables are softened, 10 minutes. Stir in reserved strained mushroom liquid and mushrooms, and cook another 2 minutes. Scrape into crockpot or soup pot, and add water or broth, bay leaf, oregano, stewed tomatoes, and barley.

Cook, covered, in crockpot, on high heat or simmered on stove until meat is tender, about 4 to $4\frac{1}{2}$ hours. Season with salt and pepper to taste. Makes 6 to 8 servings.

Creamy Rockefeller Mock Oyster Soup

You may wish to serve this soup without putting it through the blender or food processor. If so, add handfuls of bean sprouts, cilantro, and grilled chicken or beef to wispy spinach and chunks of oyster mushrooms, and you have a soup comparable to Vietnamese pho. For an interesting variation, substitute lemon thyme for thyme and lemon juice. Use caution: A little lemon thyme goes a long way. Start with $\frac{1}{8}$ teaspoon, and add by $\frac{1}{8}$-teaspoon increments.

5 tablespoons butter, divided

I small onion, minced

2 garlic cloves, minced

3 tablespoons flour

4 cups Chicken Stock (page 96)

I tablespoon lemon juice

$\frac{1}{4}$ teaspoon dried or $\frac{1}{2}$ teaspoon fresh thyme

$\frac{1}{2}$ teaspoon dried or I teaspoon fresh oregano

$\frac{1}{2}$ cup heavy cream, half-and-half, or buttermilk

7 ounces oyster mushrooms, central stems trimmed, caps cut into 1-inch slices

5 cups fresh spinach leaves (about 5 ounces)

salt and freshly ground black pepper

Parmesan cheese

In large saucepan, melt 3 tablespoons of the butter. Stir in onions and garlic and cook until softened, about 5 minutes. Whisk in flour and cook 1 minute longer. Whisk in broth, lemon juice, thyme, oregano, cream, half-and-half, or buttermilk. Bring mixture to a boil; reduce heat and simmer 5 minutes.

In large skillet, add remaining 2 tablespoons butter. Add mushrooms and cook until softened, 4 to 5 minutes. Stir mushrooms and spinach into broth. Pulse soup in food processor or blender until spinach and mushrooms are uniformly chopped into little pieces. Serve warm in bowls. Pass a chunk of Parmesan cheese and grate over each bowl. Makes 4 to 6 servings.

Mushroom Consommé with Garlic-Sage Croutons

The broth is enhanced by extracted juices from the sautéed vegetables and mushrooms. Use up odd bits and leftover mushroom stems and caps to flavor the broth of this soup. I like to serve this consommé topped with croutons and grated fontina or smoky Gouda cheese.

CONSOMMÉ

- 4 tablespoons butter
- 1 medium onion, chopped
- 2 carrots, chopped
- 2 celery stalks, chopped
- 3 garlic cloves, minced
- 1 1/2 pounds maitake or shiitake mushrooms, chopped, divided
- 8 cups water, vegetable broth, or Chicken Stock (page 96)
- 2 bay leaves
- 8 peppercorns
- 1 teaspoon dried sage, crumbled
- 1/4 cup parsley
- 2 green onions
- 1 teaspoon salt
- 1/8 teaspoon freshly ground black pepper

In large saucepan, melt butter, then add onion, carrots, celery, and garlic. Cook, stirring, until vegetables are tender, about 10 minutes. Stir in 1 pound of the mushrooms, water or broth, bay leaves, peppercorns, and sage. Bring to a boil, then reduce heat to simmer. Simmer broth for 45 minutes, until reduced and flavorful. Strain and return liquid to saucepan. Stir in remaining mushrooms, parsley, green onions, salt, and pepper. Makes 6 cups.

CROUTONS

3 tablespoons butter

2 tablespoons olive oil

**2 cups $^1/_2$-inch cubes of sliced crusty bread
or purchased bread cubes**

I garlic clove

2 teaspoons dried sage

$^1/_4$ teaspoon salt

$^1/_8$ teaspoon freshly ground black pepper

In large skillet over medium heat, heat butter and olive oil until butter is melted. Stir in bread cubes, garlic, and seasonings, and cook until bread cubes are crisp and golden, 7 to 8 minutes. Pass croutons with consommé.

Portabella mushrooms are a wonderful meat substitute for sandwiches.

Sandwiches, Wraps, and Burgers

There are countless ways to incorporate mushrooms into sandwiches, wraps, and burgers. Shiitake and portabella mushroom caps make great mock meat substitutes for vegetarians. Burgers and steak sandwiches can be embellished with melted cheese, sautéed mushrooms, and caramelized onions. Spread flavored mayonnaise on kaiser rolls, and layer with grilled mushroom caps and colorful grilled vegetables such as red peppers, eggplant slices, and red onions. Stuff a whole-wheat roll with sautéed snow peas, grilled portabella mushroom caps, blue cheese, and red onions—delicious but messy.

Make mushroom-based spreads in a food processor. Chop together mushrooms and chives, or mushrooms, roasted sweet garlic, and sun-dried tomatoes, then add cream cheese for a delicious bagel or tortilla spread.

Mushrooms combined with seafood, fish, chicken, or vegetables and grains make uniquely textured patties. The soy-scented Barley Ginger Garden Burgers are made with mushrooms, barley, and ginger. Barley adds a unique nuttiness that complements the meaty texture of any variety of mushroom. Try them or the Portabella Vegetable Burgers at your next barbecue. You can make them weeks in advance and store them in your freezer.

Cheesy Portabella Mushroom Sandwich

Shiitake, maitake, or white mushroom varieties may be used instead of portabellas. These mushroom varieties make great meat substitutes and pair well with blankets of melted cheddar, smoky Gouda, and nutty fontina cheeses.

2 thick slices bacon

4 tablespoons butter, softened

2 shallots, coarsely chopped

4 ounces portabella mushroom slices, cut into 1-inch pieces

2 kaiser rolls, cut in half

2 teaspoons garlic powder or garlic powder with parsley

1 cup grated sharp cheddar cheese

Lettuce, for garnish

Slice tomato, for garnish

Preheat broiler and place rack on top shelf of oven, about 4 inches away from heat source.

In large skillet, cook bacon until crisp. Let cool slightly, crumble into small pieces and set aside. Wipe out skillet.

Add 2 tablespoons of the butter to the skillet and stir in shallots. Cook 1 to 2 minutes until softened. Stir in mushroom slices and cook until golden, 4 to 5 minutes. Set aside.

Butter kaiser roll halves with remaining 2 tablespoons butter and sprinkle with garlic powder. Place on cookie sheet and broil until golden, about 1 minute. Remove from oven and top one half of each roll with portabella mushrooms and shallots. Sprinkle with reserved bacon and divide cheese over the two kaiser roll halves. Broil until cheese is melted.

Garnish each sandwich with lettuce and tomato. Place remaining kaiser roll half on each and serve with pickle spear and chips. Makes 2 sandwiches.

Shiitake, Red Onion, and Gorgonzola Pita Salad Pockets

Turn this recipe into a refreshing summer salad by adding a can of mandarin oranges and serving with toasted pita triangles.

DRESSING

- 1 teaspoon honey mustard
- $^1/_2$ garlic clove, minced
- 1 tablespoon balsamic vinegar
- pinch dried oregano leaves
- $^1/_8$ teaspoon salt
- $^1/_8$ teaspoon freshly ground black pepper

FOR SALAD

- 3$^1/_2$ ounces shiitake mushrooms, about eight
  2$^1/_2$-inch caps, stems trimmed off
- 2 tablespoons sliced red onion
- 3 tablespoons crumbled Gorgonzola cheese
- 1 tablespoon toasted almonds
- 3 cups mixed greens
- 2 pita pockets, sliced in half

Preheat grill. Whisk together dressing ingredients. In small bowl, toss shiitake mushroom caps with 1 tablespoon of the dressing. Grill caps, 1 to 2 minutes each side. Let cool, then slice and add to medium bowl along with onion, Gorgonzola, almonds, and lettuce. Drizzle remaining dressing over salad mixture and toss until combined. Divide mixture amongst four pita bread halves and serve. Makes 2 servings (one whole pita pocket per person).

Time-saving shortcuts

Use toasted almonds available by the package in the produce section of groceries stores.

Crumbled Gorgonzola cheese is readily available by the container in the cheese section.

Chicken Mushroom Fajitas

Instead of sautéing vegetables and chicken on the stove, grill them. Spray or brush vegetables with oil, and cook in a basket on the grill until golden brown and nicely charred around the edges. Grill whole chicken breasts about 2 minutes per side, then slice up and add to vegetables.

- **8 ounces cream cheese, softened**
- **I teaspoon fajita seasoning**
- **I tablespoon chopped fresh cilantro**
- **$1/_2$ teaspoon garlic powder**
- **4 tablespoons oil, divided**
- **4 ounces exotic or wild mushrooms, such as crimini, shiitake, oyster, or portabella, sliced**
- **I small red onion, thinly sliced**
- **I green bell pepper, thinly sliced**
- **I red bell pepper, thinly sliced**
- **$1/_2$ teaspoon salt**
- **2 boneless, skinless chicken breasts, thinly sliced crosswise into strips**
- **4 8-inch flour tortillas**

In small bowl, stir together cream cheese, fajita seasoning, cilantro, and garlic powder. Set aside.

In large heavy skillet over moderately high heat, heat 1 tablespoon of the oil. Sauté mushrooms until softened and liquid has evaporated, 3 to 4 minutes. Scrape into medium bowl and set aside.

In same skillet over moderately high heat, heat 2 tablespoons of the oil. Add onion, peppers, and salt and sauté until crisp-tender, about 4 minutes. Scrape into bowl with mushrooms.

Heat remaining 1 tablespoon of oil in skillet and add chicken. Cook over moderately high heat until just opaque throughout, about 2 minutes. Toss with vegetables and heat through.

Place tortillas on a microwavable plate and microwave about 15 seconds on high, until warmed through. Divide cream cheese mixture into four portions and spread over each tortilla. Spoon chicken and vegetables over cream cheese, roll up, and serve. Makes 4 fajitas.

Time-saving shortcut

Substitute precooked strips of chicken breast meat. Reheat in microwave and stir into cooked vegetables.

Portabella, Roasted Red Pepper, and Goat Cheese Focaccia Wedges

Olive tapenade is available at gourmet kitchen shops and specialty food stores.

3 4-inch-diameter portabella mushroom caps (about 6 ounces), cut in $1/_4$-inch slices

1 tablespoon red wine vinegar

5 tablespoons olive oil, divided

$1/_2$ teaspoon dried rosemary

1 recipe Parmesan Pepper Focaccia (page 94)

2 ounces goat cheese, room temperature

2 ounces cream cheese, room temperature

$1/_2$ cup prepared olive tapenade

2 roasted red, green, orange, or yellow peppers, cut in 1-inch slices (see page 102)

1 small red onion, cut into paper-thin slices

Preheat broiler. On a greased cookie sheet (or line with foil and coat with cooking spray), line up portabella mushroom slices. In small bowl, stir together vinegar, 3 tablespoons of the olive oil, and rosemary. Drizzle over mushroom slices. Grill or broil mushroom caps until cooked through, about 4 minutes. Set aside to cool slightly.

Slice focaccia open, place the two halves on cookie sheet, and brush remaining 2 tablespoons of olive oil over each cut side. Broil 4 inches from heat for 3 to 4 minutes, until golden brown. Let cool.

In small bowl, combine goat cheese and cream cheese. Smear on one half of the cut-side-up focaccia. Spread olive tapenade over the other half. Layer peppers, mushrooms, and raw onion slices over tapenade. Place cheese-covered focaccia half over top, and cut into 8 sandwich wedges. Makes 8 servings.

Time-saving shortcuts

Check in the bakery section of your local supermarket for freshly baked focaccia.

Roasted peppers are available at the supermarket in jars or from the deli.

Portabella Vegetable Burgers with Basil Yogurt Sauce

These colorful veggie burgers freeze well. Keep extra patties in your freezer for barbecue guests who request vegetarian in place of grilled beef patties.

> **3 tablespoons olive oil**
> **I cup chopped onion (about I small onion)**
> **I carrot, chopped**
> **I sweet bell pepper, red, orange, or yellow, chopped**
> **2 portabella mushroom caps (about 8 ounces), stems trimmed, chopped**
> **I garlic clove, minced**
> **I cup cooked barley (regular or quick-cooking)**
> **I egg**
> **$^{1}/_{2}$ cup shredded Parmesan cheese**
> **$^{3}/_{4}$ teaspoon salt**
> **pinch cayenne pepper**

Preheat broiler. Line a cookie sheet with foil. Grease foil (you can spray 6 spots on foil where you will be placing patties).

In large nonstick skillet over moderate heat, heat 2 tablespoons of the oil. Stir in onion, carrot, and bell pepper, and cook until tender, 5 to 6 minutes. Scrape into medium bowl.

Add remaining 1 tablespoon of oil to skillet, and sauté mushrooms and garlic until liquid has evaporated, about 5 minutes. Scrape into bowl with vegetables. Let cool slightly, then stir in barley, egg, cheese, salt, and cayenne pepper.

Using a $^{1}/_{3}$-cup measuring cup, scoop out mixture (it will be wet) and place on prepared foil, forming 6 patties. Broil patties 5 inches from heat source, until browned on one side. Carefully turn patties over (they will be delicate), and brown 5 minutes on other side.

Allow to cool slightly; patties will firm up as they cool on cookie sheet. Serve warm on rolls or alone, topped with Basil Yogurt Sauce. Makes 6 burgers.

BASIL YOGURT SAUCE

$1/4$ cup plain yogurt
3 tablespoons mayonnaise
I teaspoon lemon juice
I tablespoon chopped fresh basil

In small bowl, stir together all ingredients until combined. Makes $1/2$ cup sauce.

Barley Ginger Garden Burgers
with Lemon Dill Sauce

These moist, flavorful vegetarian patties freeze well in Ziploc freezer bags. Reheat patties in the microwave on high for 1 to 2 minutes. Crimini or trumpet mushrooms can be used instead of shiitake. If you can't find mushroom soy sauce, you can substitute regular soy sauce.

> **2 tablespoons olive oil**
> **$1/_2$ pound shiitake mushrooms, sliced**
> **I red pepper, chopped (about I cup)**
> **$1/_2$ cup chopped green onions (about 6)**
> **I teaspoon freshly grated ginger root**
> **I tablespoon mushroom soy sauce (page 102)**
> **$1/_2$ teaspoon ground cumin**
> **I teaspoon lemon juice**
> **I cup cooked barley (quick-cooking)**
> **I egg**
> **$1/_3$ cup grated Parmesan cheese**
> **I cup fresh breadcrumbs**
> **$1/_4$ teaspoon salt**
> **$1/_4$ teaspoon freshly ground black pepper**

Preheat oven to 500 degrees. Line a cookie sheet with foil. Grease or spray foil with vegetable oil. Set aside.

In large skillet over moderate heat, heat olive oil. Stir in mushrooms and red pepper, and cook until crisp-tender, about 5 to 6 minutes. Stir in green onions, and cook 1 minute longer. Remove from heat, and mix in ginger, soy sauce, cumin, and lemon juice. Let mixture cool slightly.

Scrape mushroom mixture into food processor. Pulse until mushrooms and vegetables are finely chopped. Scrape mixture into medium bowl, and stir in barley, egg, Parmesan cheese, breadcrumbs, salt, and pepper. Using $1/_2$-cup measuring cup, scoop out and form 6 patties, spacing evenly on prepared cookie sheet (mixture will be wet).

Broil patties 5 inches from broiler, about 5 minutes per side, until golden. Let cool slightly. Serve warm on rolls or alone, topped or with Lemon Dill Sauce. Makes 6 burgers.

LEMON DILL SAUCE

- $^1/_4$ **cup plain yogurt**
- **3 tablespoons mayonnaise**
- **1 teaspoon lemon juice**
- **1 teaspoon freshly chopped or**
  $^1/_2$ teaspoon dried dill

In small bowl, stir together all ingredients until combined. Makes about $^1/_2$ cup sauce.

Sauteed mushrooms and onions are the salt and pepper of the steak world.

Main Courses

In this selection of main courses, the diversity of mushrooms shines through. They're threaded on skewers, incorporated in pasta and potpie, grilled, baked, and used as a cushion for tenderloin.

Shiitake, crimini, and portabella mushrooms keep their shape when sliced and quickly sautéed in stir-fries, or when skewered and added to the grill along with other vegetables, meats, or seafood. Brush Vinaigrette Marinade (page 101) over mushrooms before grilling to accentuate the natural juiciness of whole caps and slices.

Flank Steak with Grilled Vegetables and Mushrooms

Feel free to try this recipe using different garden-fresh vegetables. Also, shiitake mushrooms are just as wonderful on the grill as portabellas. Slip a few shiitake caps into the lineup for a rich, woodsy flavor.

> 1 tablespoon Dijon mustard
>
> 3 tablespoons red wine vinegar
>
> 1 garlic clove, minced
>
> 1 tablespoon brown sugar
>
> 1 tablespoon ketchup
>
> 1 tablespoon Worcestershire sauce
>
> 1 teaspoon dried or 2 teaspoons fresh tarragon
>
> $1/_2$ teaspoon salt
>
> $1/_4$ teaspoon freshly ground black pepper
>
> $1/_2$ cup plus 3 tablespoons olive oil, divided
>
> $1 1/_2$ pounds flank steak, trimmed
>
> 1 summer squash, sliced diagonally into thin strips
>
> 1 zucchini, sliced diagonally into thin strips
>
> 1 red onion, thickly sliced (don't separate rings)
>
> 6 ounces portabella mushrooms (about 3)
>
> 1 tablespoon chopped fresh parsley or cilantro

In small bowl, make marinade by whisking together mustard, vinegar, garlic, brown sugar, ketchup, Worcestershire, tarragon, salt, and pepper. Gradually whisk in $1/_2$ cup of the olive oil. Place flank steak in a shallow pan, and pour all but 4 tablespoons of marinade over the meat. Cover and let marinate, turning occasionally, for 1 hour at room temperature or overnight in the refrigerator.

Preheat grill. Brush summer squash and zucchini strips, red onion slices, and portabella mushroom caps with remaining 3 tablespoons oil. Grill mushroom caps until golden, about 3 minutes per side, and other vegetables until crisp-tender. Remove vegetables to medium bowl. Using a fork, separate grilled onion rings and combine with squashes. Let mushrooms cool slightly, then cut each cap into thick slices and add to bowl with vegetables. Toss with 2 tablespoons of the reserved vinaigrette and chopped parsley or cilantro.

Grill flank steak 4 to 5 minutes per side for medium rare. Place on platter, drizzle with remaining 2 tablespoons of the vinaigrette, and let rest 10 minutes. Transfer steak to carving board and slice across the grain on a diagonal into thin strips. Serve on plate next to grilled vegetables. Makes 4 servings.

Chicken Drumsticks with Spinach, Lentils, and Shiitake Mushrooms

This robust, lentil-laced chicken dish is prepared and presented in the same skillet.

4 chicken drumsticks (remove skin if desired)

flour seasoned with salt and pepper

I tablespoon oil

3 cups Chicken Stock (page 96) or Beef Broth (page 97)

$^3/_4$ cup dry lentils, picked through and rinsed

I tablespoon butter

$^1/_2$ pound fresh shiitake mushrooms, stems removed and caps sliced

2 garlic cloves, minced

4 cups fresh spinach leaves (about 4 ounces)

$^1/_4$ cup grated smoked Gouda cheese

Dredge drumsticks in seasoned flour. In large heavy skillet, heat the oil. Add drumsticks and brown on all sides about 8 minutes. Stir in chicken broth and lentils. Bring liquid to a boil, then reduce heat, cover, and simmer until chicken is cooked through and lentils are tender, about 15 minutes. Remove from heat.

In the meantime, in large skillet over moderate heat, melt butter. Add mushrooms and garlic, and sauté until mushrooms are tender, about 3 minutes. Carefully pile spinach over top of chicken, cover, and let steam until leaves are wilted, about 2 minutes. Gently toss spinach, mushrooms, and garlic into lentils and around chicken pieces. Sprinkle with cheese and serve immediately. Makes 2 to 4 servings.

Time-saving shortcut

Substitute canned broth for homemade.

Baked Cheesy Chicken Ravioli

This creamy pasta dish is best spooned into wide-brimmed bowls. You'll want to pass a basket of warm, crusty bread slices to mop up the delicious sauce. Complete the meal by serving a light salad too. Substituting maitake, shiitake, trumpet, or oyster mushrooms would add a different dimension to the dish. Try a combination of any of these mushrooms.

> **doubled recipe Cream Sauce (page 98)**
> **9-ounce package fresh or frozen four-cheese ravioli**
> **3 cups grilled or baked chicken, cut into $1/_2$-by-2-inch strips**
> **$1/_4$ cup thin-sliced green onions or 1-inch lengths of snipped chives**
> **2 tablespoons butter**
> **3 cups sliced crimini mushrooms (about 8 ounces)**
> **1 garlic clove, minced**
> **$1/_2$ teaspoon crumbled dried oregano**
> **$1/_4$ teaspoon salt**
> **$1/_8$ teaspoon pepper**
> **1 $1/_4$ cups grated sharp cheddar cheese**

Preheat oven to 350 degrees. Butter or spray with oil a 12-by-9-by-3-inch gratin dish, either oval or square. Prepare Cream Sauce and set aside.

In large pot of boiling salted water, cook ravioli according to package directions. Drain well, then scatter evenly into prepared baking pan. Distribute cooked chicken and green onions or chives among ravioli.

In large skillet over moderately high heat, melt butter. Add mushrooms, garlic, oregano, salt, and pepper, and sauté until liquid evaporates and mushrooms are tender, 6 to 8 minutes. Fold mushrooms evenly throughout ravioli mixture. Sprinkle shredded cheese over ravioli. Bake in middle of oven for 25 to 30 minutes, or until hot and bubbly. Makes 4 servings.

Time-saving shortcuts

Use commercially available pregrilled or baked fresh or frozen chicken strips.

Use 2 16-ounce jars of Alfredo sauce in place of homemade Cream Sauce.

Spicy Parmesan-Crusted Tilapia with Mushrooms and Spinach

You can make this tasty, crispy recipe with catfish instead of tilapia.

$^1/_2$ cup cornmeal

$^1/_4$ cup plus 2 tablespoons grated Parmesan cheese, divided

1 tablespoon Southwestern seasoning

$^1/_4$ teaspoon salt

1 egg

2 tablespoons flour

4 tilapia fillets (1 to 1 $^1/_2$ pounds total)

2 tablespoons olive oil

3 tablespoons butter, divided

1 garlic clove, minced

1 shallot, minced

4 ounces exotic mushrooms, such as trumpet, crimini, or oyster, sliced

10-ounce package frozen spinach, thawed, chopped, and squeezed of excess liquid

2 tablespoons fresh lemon juice

In medium shallow bowl, combine cornmeal, $^1/_4$ cup Parmesan cheese, Southwestern seasoning, and salt. Put egg in another shallow bowl, and stir with fork. Place flour in a third shallow bowl. Dredge fillets first in flour, then egg, and then coat all over with the cornmeal mixture.

In large skillet, heat olive oil and 1 tablespoon butter. Fry fish in batches until golden brown on both sides, about 3 minutes per side. Set fillets on serving platter and cover loosely with foil. Wipe out skillet with paper towel.

In same skillet, heat remaining 2 tablespoons of butter. Stir in garlic, shallot, and mushrooms, and cook 3 to 4 minutes, until tender. Add spinach and cook until liquid evaporates, 4 to 5 minutes. Stir in remaining 2 tablespoons Parmesan cheese and lemon juice. Season with salt and pepper. Place each fish fillet on top of mushroom-spinach mixture and serve. Makes 4 servings.

Italian Sausages, Peppers, and Mushrooms over Polenta

Feel free to omit polenta and serve this mixture slathered over a toasted hoagie or sub roll.

2 tablespoons olive oil

3 tablespoons water

6 sweet Italian sausages or I long sausage (about I $1/4$ pounds)

I medium sweet onion, thinly sliced

I garlic clove, minced

2 red, yellow, or orange bell peppers, cut into $1/4$-inch julienne strips

$1/2$ pound crimini or white mushrooms, quartered

2 tablespoons balsamic vinegar

I tablespoon chopped Italian parsley

$1/2$ teaspoon dried oregano

$1/2$ cup homemade or store-bought tomato sauce

salt and pepper to taste

I recipe Polenta (page 95)

$1/2$ cup shredded mozzarella cheese

To large heavy skillet, add 1 tablespoon olive oil, water, and sausage. Cover pan and cook over moderate heat, turning once, 15 to 20 minutes. Remove cover and cook until golden-brown. (Alternatively, sausages may be pricked all over with a fork and then broiled or grilled until cooked through.) Transfer sausage to a platter and slice into 1-inch thick pieces. Cover and keep warm.

Add remaining 1 tablespoon of oil to pan. Over moderately high heat, sauté onion, garlic, peppers, and mushrooms until tender, about 5 minutes. Stir in vinegar, parsley, oregano, and tomato sauce. Bring to a boil and simmer about 2 minutes. Season sauce with salt and pepper.

Make Polenta recipe or cut store-bought tube into 6 $1/2$-inch slices. Heat slices in microwave until warm throughout, about 1 minute. Put sliced sausages on polenta triangles or rounds, and top with pepper sauce. Sprinkle mozzarella cheese over each portion. Makes 6 servings.

Time-saving shortcut

Polenta is widely available in the produce section at the supermarket.
    Look for 1-pound tubes.

Gorgonzola Tenderloin on Tarragon Portabella Cushions

This fast but elegant dish embellishes any fancy occasion. It's delicious grilled or pan-fried. In hot weather, serve this luscious combination of meat and mushrooms over a bed of tender mixed greens. For a heavier wintry meal, accompany with buttered noodles or rice.

1 tablespoon Dijon mustard

$^1/_2$ teaspoon minced garlic

$^1/_2$ teaspoon fresh or $^1/_4$ teaspoon dried tarragon

2 tablespoons red wine vinegar

$^1/_4$ teaspoon salt

$^1/_8$ teaspoon freshly ground pepper

$^1/_4$ cup plus 2 tablespoons olive oil

2 beef tenderloins, about 1 $^1/_2$ inches thick (about $^3/_4$ pound)

2 portabella mushroom caps (about 3 ounces each), stems trimmed even with caps

1 ounce (about $^1/_4$ cup) Gorgonzola cheese, crumbled

1 tablespoon chopped fresh parsley, for garnish

Preheat broiler. In small bowl, whisk together mustard, garlic, tarragon, vinegar, salt, and pepper. In a steady stream, whisk in olive oil until blended. Set aside 2 tablespoons of this vinaigrette.

Place tenderloins and mushroom caps on a plate. Brush remaining vinaigrette over meat and caps. In cast-iron skillet over moderately high heat, pan-fry mushrooms until softened, 3 to 4 minutes per side. Remove and set aside. Then pan-fry beef tenderloins to desired doneness (3 to 4 minutes per side for medium rare). Carefully slide a mushroom cap under each tenderloin in skillet, and top with Gorgonzola cheese.

Broil tenderloins in top third of oven, about 4 inches from heat source, until cheese begins to melt, about 2 minutes. Remove from oven and drizzle reserved vinaigrette over top of tenderloins. Sprinkle with chopped parsley and serve. Makes 2 servings.

Grilled Shrimp and Shiitake Mushroom Kabobs

Play around with different fish and mushroom combinations using this zesty marinade. Try substituting 1 pound fresh tuna chunks, 1 pound portabella mushroom chunks, and wedges of purple onion.

$1/2$ **cup lime juice (from about 3 limes)**

$1/3$ **cup soy sauce**

$1/4$ **cup olive oil**

$1/4$ **cup dark brown sugar**

2 tablespoons chopped fresh chives

2 garlic cloves, minced

$1/2$ **teaspoon salt**

pinch crushed red pepper flakes

1 pound large shrimp, shelled and deveined

10 ounces shiitake mushrooms, stems removed and caps wiped clean

1 pound cherry tomatoes, or 1 U.S. dry pint grape tomatoes

1 tablespoon chopped fresh cilantro or Italian parsley

In shallow pan, soak about 6 or 8 12-inch bamboo skewers in water for 30 minutes. Remove from water and set aside. Preheat grill or broiler.

In small bowl, combine lime juice, soy sauce, olive oil, brown sugar, chives, garlic, salt, and pepper flakes. Place shrimp in another bowl and sprinkle with $1/2$ cup of this marinade. In a third bowl, combine mushrooms and tomatoes, and sprinkle with $1/2$ cup of marinade. Thread shrimp, tomatoes, and mushrooms decoratively onto 12-inch bamboo skewers. Let marinate about 10 minutes (longer, and the shrimp will begin to "cook" in the lime juice).

Grill or broil kabobs about 4 inches from heat source for 3 to 4 minutes, turning once if grilling, until shrimp is pink throughout. Remove from grill or broiler and sprinkle with remaining marinade and cilantro or parsley. Makes 4 to 6 servings.

Herbed Parmesan Veal Roast with Exotic Mushrooms

Delicately flavored oyster mushrooms, Worcestershire sauce, and parsley perfume this robust veal roast. It can be sliced and served at room temperature, which makes it an ideal candidate for an elegant luncheon buffet.

3–4 pound boneless veal shoulder roast, butterflied

I garlic clove, minced

2 tablespoons Worcestershire sauce

$^1/_2$ teaspoon freshly ground black pepper, divided

2 tablespoons chopped fresh parsley, divided

$^1/_4$ cup grated Parmesan cheese

$^3/_4$ cup fresh breadcrumbs

$^1/_4$ teaspoon salt

I $^1/_4$ cups sliced oyster or trumpet mushrooms

2 tablespoons olive oil

In large glass dish, lay veal out flat and rub all over with garlic. Sprinkle both sides with Worcestershire sauce, half the pepper, and half the parsley. Cover and refrigerate 1 to 2 hours or overnight.

Preheat oven to 450 degrees. In small bowl, combine remaining parsley and pepper, Parmesan cheese, breadcrumbs, and salt.

Lay veal out flat on a work surface. Press half of breadcrumb mixture over veal. Arrange mushroom slices over top of breadcrumbs. Press remaining breadcrumbs over mushrooms. Roll up veal and secure with kitchen string to form a neat package.

In large cast-iron or other ovenproof skillet over moderately high heat, heat olive oil. Sear roast until browned on all sides, about 15 minutes. Cover loosely with foil and place in middle of oven. After 10 minutes, turn oven temperature down to 350 degrees and cook for another hour and a half, until roast reaches an internal temperature of 150–155 degrees. Remove roast from oven and let rest for 15 minutes. Remove string and carve. Makes 4 to 6 servings.

Succulent Short Ribs in Tomato-Chickpea Sauce

This dish may be prepared a day ahead, cooked for the first 2 hours, allowed to cool, and refrigerated. About an hour before serving, scrape off any hardened fat, and stir in cilantro, lemon juice, and ginger. Slowly reheat on stove or in 350-degree oven until warmed throughout. Pass around a basket of warm, crusty bread slices to mop up the stewlike sauce.

I teaspoon cumin

2 teaspoons paprika

I teaspoon allspice

I teaspoon salt

$1/_4$ teaspoon freshly ground black pepper

3 pounds short ribs (with about 8 2- to 3-inch ribs)

2 tablespoons oil, divided

I medium onion, chopped

$1^3/_4$ cups Chicken Stock (page 96) or Beef Broth (page 97)

$14^1/_2$-ounce can diced tomatoes with juice

$14^1/_2$-ounce can chickpeas, drained

10 ounces whole white, beech, or crimini mushrooms

2 tablespoons lemon juice

$1/_4$ cup chopped fresh cilantro

I tablespoon grated fresh or I teaspoon dried ginger

Preheat oven to 375 degrees. Cut short ribs between bones into single rib pieces and trim excess fat. In small bowl, combine cumin, paprika, allspice, salt, and pepper.

Rub ribs all over with spice mixture.

In 6- to 8-quart Dutch oven or ovenproof casserole over moderately high heat, heat 1 tablespoon of the oil, and add as many ribs as will fit into pan. Brown on all sides, then drain on paper towels. Repeat with remaining ribs, adding more oil if necessary. Remove ribs. Add remaining 1 tablespoon of oil to skillet, and sauté onion until softened, about 5 minutes. Stir in broth, tomatoes, chickpeas, mushrooms, and ribs. Bring mixture to a boil then remove from heat. Cover casserole loosely with foil and place in oven.

Braise ribs, turning once. After two hours of cooking, stir in lemon juice, cilantro, and ginger. Cook ribs until tender, about 30 to 45 minutes longer. Serve in big bowls over steamed rice or alongside buttered noodles. Makes 4 servings.

Time-saving shortcut

Substitute a 14½-ounce can of chicken or beef broth for homemade.

Creamy Chicken Piccata

Serve this succulent chicken recipe with buttered noodles or crispy-fried sliced potatoes.

6–8 boneless, skinless, thin-sliced chicken breasts (about 1½ pounds)

1 tablespoon butter or margarine

3 tablespoons olive oil, divided

2 tablespoons lemon juice, divided

2 cups loosely packed exotic mushrooms, such as crimini, shiitake, chanterelle, or trumpet, quartered or sliced (about 4 ounces)

1 large shallot, finely chopped

½ cup white wine

1 cup chicken broth, reserving 2 tablespoons

2 tablespoons heavy cream

2 teaspoons cornstarch

2 tablespoons capers, rinsed and drained

2 tablespoons chopped parsley

In large heavy skillet over moderately high heat, sauté chicken breasts in butter and 2 tablespoons of the oil until golden brown and opaque throughout, 2 to 3 minutes per side. Remove to a warm serving platter. Sprinkle 1 tablespoon of the lemon juice over cooked chicken and cover loosely with foil.

Add remaining 1 tablespoon of olive oil to skillet over moderate heat. Add mushrooms and shallots, and sauté until tender, about 5 minutes. Stir in white wine and cook until wine is reduced by half, about 3 minutes. Whisk in chicken broth. In small cup, combine reserved 2 tablespoons of chicken broth and cornstarch. Whisk into skillet and bring to a boil. Stir in cream, capers, and remaining 1 tablespoon of lemon juice, and cook 1 minute longer. Remove sauce from heat and pour over chicken. Sprinkle with parsley and serve. Makes 3 to 4 servings.

Salmon with Chinese Noodles, Straw Mushrooms, and Vegetables

Fresh Chinese-style noodles are found in 9-ounce packages near egg roll and wonton wrappers in the refrigerated section of the produce department. Angel hair pasta can be substituted.

2 garlic cloves, minced

**1 teaspoon freshly grated and chopped or
$1/_2$ teaspoon ground ginger**

2 tablespoons rice vinegar

$1/_2$ cup plus 2 tablespoons oyster sauce

1 tablespoon soy sauce

1 tablespoon sesame oil

3 tablespoons olive oil, divided

pinch crushed red pepper flakes

salt and black pepper to taste

**9-ounce package fresh Chinese noodles or
angel hair pasta**

**$1 1/_2$ cups oyster mushrooms, sliced
(about $3 1/_2$ ounces)**

**4 ounces snow peas, sliced diagonally into thirds
(about 1 cup)**

6 green onions, sliced (about $1/_3$ cup)

$1 1/_2$ tablespoons toasted sesame seeds

4 to 6 salmon fillets (about 2 pounds)

2 tablespoons fresh cilantro, chopped

Preheat oven to 375 degrees. In small bowl, whisk together garlic, ginger, vinegar, oyster sauce, soy sauce, sesame oil, 2 tablespoons of the olive oil, red pepper flakes, salt, and pepper.

Cook noodles or pasta according to package directions. Drain well. Transfer to large bowl and toss with $1/_2$ cup of the sauce.

In large heavy ovenproof skillet over moderately high heat, heat remaining 1 tablespoon olive oil. Stir in mushrooms, snow peas, and green onions. Cook, stirring, until vegetables are crisp-tender, 2 to 3 minutes. Season with salt and pepper. Toss in with the pasta along with toasted sesame seeds.

Place salmon fillets in 9 x 13 baking dish and coat with remaining sauce. Bake in oven until opaque throughout, 14 to 16 minutes. Serve warm salmon on dinner plates next to portion of Chinese noodles. Sprinkle both with fresh cilantro. Makes 4 to 6 servings.

Time-saving shortcut

Substitute a 15-ounce can peeled whole straw mushrooms, packed in water, drained, for the sliced oyster mushrooms.

Country Ham Slices with Creamy Shiitake Gravy

This Southern-style dish cries out for buttermilk biscuits and sautéed greens.

3 tablespoons butter, divided
4 ham slices, $^1/_2$ inch thick (about 2 pounds)
2 shallots, minced (about $^1/_2$ cup)
2 cups sliced shiitake mushroom caps (about 7 ounces)
2 tablespoons sweet sherry
1 $^1/_2$ teaspoons chopped fresh or 1 teaspoon dried sage
1 recipe Cream Sauce (page 98)
1 tablespoon chopped fresh parsley

In large heavy skillet over moderate heat, melt 1 tablespoon of the butter. Working in batches, fry 2 ham slices at a time until lightly browned on each side, about 3 to 5 minutes per side. Repeat with remaining ham and another 1 tablespoon of the butter. Transfer to a platter and cover loosely with foil.

In same skillet over moderate heat, melt remaining 1 tablespoon of butter. Stir in shallots and mushrooms, and sauté until mushrooms are softened, about 5 minutes. Add sherry and sage, and cook 1 minute longer.

Prepare Cream Sauce. Stir mushroom mixture into sauce. Spoon over ham slices and sprinkle with parsley. Pass any leftover sauce. Makes 4 servings.

Shrimp, Shiitake, and Asparagus Risotto

Garnish each serving of risotto with fresh Parmesan shavings. Use a vegetable peeler to slice thin shavings of cheese over the top of each bowl.

6 cups Chicken Stock (page 96)

I pound uncooked large shrimp, peeled and deveined

4 tablespoons olive oil, divided

I bunch asparagus (about I¼ pounds), ends trimmed and sliced on the diagonal into I½-inch pieces

½ pound shiitake mushrooms, stems removed, caps brushed clean with damp paper towel, and thickly sliced

2 tablespoons soy sauce

I small onion, chopped

2 garlic cloves, minced

I½ cups uncooked arborio rice (about 9½ ounces)

⅔ cup dry vermouth or white wine

½ cup grated Parmesan cheese, plus additional cheese to pass

3 tablespoons chopped fresh cilantro or parsley (optional)

salt and pepper to taste

In 2-quart saucepan, bring chicken broth to a boil. Stir in shrimp and simmer until opaque throughout, about 2 minutes. Remove pan from heat. Using slotted spoon, remove shrimp to a medium bowl, cover, and set aside. Strain broth, then cover and keep warm.

In large skillet over moderately high heat, heat 2 tablespoons of the olive oil. Add asparagus and sauté until crisp-tender, about 4 minutes. Scrape into bowl with shrimp.

In same skillet over moderately high heat, add 1 tablespoon of the olive oil, and cook shiitake mushroom slices until limp and golden, 2 to 3 minutes. Scrape into bowl with shrimp and asparagus. Toss shrimp mixture with soy sauce, cover, and set aside.

In same skillet over moderately high heat, add remaining 1 tablespoon olive oil. Stir in onion and cook until tender, about 5 minutes. Add garlic and cook 1 minute longer. Stir in rice and cook until edges are translucent, about 2 minutes. Add wine and cook, stirring, until liquid is absorbed. Stir in 1 cup of reserved warm broth, and cook over moderate heat until liquid is absorbed. Continue to add broth 1 cup at a time, cooking until rice is tender and all of the broth is incorporated, 25 to 30 minutes. Fold in shrimp mixture, ½ cup Parmesan cheese, and chopped cilantro or parsley, if desired. Season to taste with salt and pepper. Serve immediately. Pass additional Parmesan cheese. Makes 4 to 6 servings.

Time-saving shortcut

Substitute canned low-salt chicken broth for the homemade stock.

Cornish Game Hens with Lemon Pesto Stuffing

To sear in juices and add smoky flavor, grill the birds, turning on all sides, for 10 minutes, then place in 350-degree oven and bake for 20 to 25 minutes. If you are grilling the birds, secure the openings with toothpicks that have been soaked in water for 20 minutes or metal skewers. Otherwise, the stuffing tends to leak out, especially when you turn the birds.

One whole bird may be too big for smaller appetites. The hens are easy to split in half lengthwise with a sharp knife once they have been cooked.

> **3 Cornish game hens about 1 $^1/_4$ pounds each, rinsed and patted dry with paper towels**
>
> **garlic salt**
>
> **pepper**
>
> **1 recipe Lemon Pesto Stuffing (page 93), cut recipe in half**
>
> **6 tablespoons butter, melted, plus 1 teaspoon**
>
> **$^1/_2$ cup dry red wine**

Preheat grill or heat oven to 425 degrees. Sprinkle hens liberally inside and out with garlic salt and pepper. Loosely pack each hen with stuffing and place in greased, shallow roasting pan. Leave some space around each bird. Roast in oven or grill for 10 minutes. Brush hens with 3 tablespoons of melted butter. Reduce heat to 350 degrees and continue to bake, basting with 3 tablespoons melted butter until juices run clear when thigh is pierced with a knife, 25 to 30 minutes. If grilling, you will need to turn birds when basting.

Remove hens from roasting pan. Add wine to pan and bring to a boil over high heat, stirring to scrape up any browned bits from the bottom of pan. Cook for 1 minute and then strain sauce into small bowl or serving dish. Stir in remaining 1 teaspoon butter and pass with Cornish hens. Makes 3 to 6 servings.

Penne Mushroom Vegetable Pasta

Use this recipe as a base on which to build. Add grilled chicken, shrimp, or strips of beef to turn this pasta dish into a substantial meal. Toss in fresh garden herbs for additional flavor, or incorporate grilled portabella or shiitake mushroom caps into the pasta for a more robust dish. Smoked Gouda or fontina cheese may be substituted for Parmesan.

DRESSING

$1/4$ cup white balsamic or white wine vinegar
2 tablespoons honey mustard
1 garlic clove, minced
$1/2$ teaspoon salt
$1/2$ teaspoon freshly ground black pepper
$2/3$ cup extra-virgin olive oil

In small bowl, whisk together vinegar, mustard, garlic, salt, and pepper. Slowly drizzle in olive oil. Set aside.

PASTA

3 tablespoons extra-virgin olive oil, divided
10-ounce package crimini mushrooms, quartered (about 3 cups)
1 small red onion, thinly sliced
1 small summer squash, sliced and quartered
1 zucchini, thinly sliced and quartered
1 small tomato, diced
12-ounce jar marinated artichoke hearts, quartered
4 quarts salted water
1 pound penne pasta
$1/2$ cup shredded basil leaves
$1/2$ cup grated Parmesan cheese

In large nonstick skillet over moderately high heat, heat 2 tablespoons of the olive oil. Stir in mushrooms and cook until tender and liquid evaporates, about 8 minutes. Scrape into large serving bowl.

In same skillet, sauté onions in remaining 1 tablespoon of oil. Cook over moderate heat until tender. Stir in summer squash and zucchini, and cook until crisp-tender, about 5 minutes. Stir in tomato and artichoke hearts, and cook 1 minute longer. Scrape into serving bowl with mushrooms.

In large saucepan, bring 4 quarts salted water to rolling boil. Add pasta and cook until al dente, 12 to 15 minutes. Drain well, then toss in serving bowl with vegetables. Toss in dressing, basil, and Parmesan cheese. Serve hot or at room temperature. Makes 8 to 10 servings.

Grilled New York Strip Steak with Portabella Mushroom Slices

All that's missing are sliced and sautéed or grilled golden onions.

- **2 New York strip steaks (about 1 pound)**
- **1 garlic clove, minced**
- **1 tablespoon Montreal Steak Seasoning**
- **2 tablespoons olive oil**
- **1 recipe Grilled Portabella Mushroom Slices (page 86)**

Place steaks in glass baking pan and rub with garlic. Sprinkle with Montreal seasoning and oil. Let marinate at room temperature for up to 1 hour, or cover and refrigerate overnight.

Preheat grill. Grill steaks to desired doneness (about 4 minutes per side for medium rare depending on thickness), and serve along with Grilled Portabella Mushroom Slices. Makes 2 servings.

Crown Roast of Pork with Porcini Mushroom Stuffing

Showcase this elegant centerpiece at your next buffet. The filling may be made a couple days in advance. Have the butcher trim and tie together 2 racks of center-cut pork loin chops to form a ring.

9 1/2-pound center-cut pork loin roast, formed in a crown

I ounce dried porcini mushrooms

1/2 cup warm water

I tablespoon butter

I medium onion, chopped

8 ounces crimini, white, portabella, shiitake, or maitake mushrooms, sliced

3 garlic cloves, minced

1 1/2 cups fresh, blanched spinach, or 2 10-ounce packages frozen spinach, thawed (squeeze out excess liquid and chop)

1 1/2 cups fresh breadcrumbs

1/2 cup grated Parmesan cheese

2 eggs

2 tablespoons parsley, chopped

1/2 teaspoon salt

1/4 teaspoon freshly ground black pepper

2 tablespoons olive oil

3/4 cup white wine

I cup water or Chicken Stock (page 96)

1–2 tablespoons flour

Preheat oven to 350 degrees. Place roast in large roasting pan. Soak porcini mushrooms in 1/2 cup warm water until softened, about 15 minutes. Remove and chop. Strain and reserve soaking liquid.

In large skillet over moderately high heat, melt butter. Sauté onions until softened, about 5 minutes. Stir in sliced mushrooms, porcini mushrooms, and garlic. Cook 2 minutes longer, until excess moisture has evaporated. Scrape into large bowl and let cool.

Add spinach, breadcrumbs, Parmesan cheese, eggs, parsley, salt, and pepper to mushroom mixture and combine well. Spoon into center of roast and cover loosely with buttered foil. Place a ring of foil over chop ends. Brush roast with oil, add wine to pan, and cook for about 3 hours, until thermometer registers 155 degrees. Add more wine to pan to prevent scorching during cooking, if necessary. Remove foil ring last 30 minutes of cooking. When done, carefully remove roast from pan, and let rest 10 to 15 minutes before carving. Meanwhile, place roasting pan over moderate heat, and bring juices, strained reserved porcini mushroom liquid, and 1 cup water or chicken broth to a boil. Whisk in flour until desired consistency. Simmer and cook 1 more minute. Pour sauce into gravy boat. Carve roast, cutting between each chop, and serve along with a portion of stuffing. Pass gravy. Makes 10 to 12 servings.

Herbed Crusted Pork Chops with Crumbed Zucchini-Mushroom Ragout

This dish is reminiscent of a pork Wiener schnitzel. Make sure to accompany each pork chop with a lemon wedge to accentuate the herb flavors.

$^2/_3$ **cup fresh breadcrumbs**

$^1/_4$ **cup grated Parmesan cheese**

2 tablespoons freshly chopped flat-leaf Italian parsley

I egg, beaten

**4 thin-cut, boneless, center-cut pork chops
   (just under I pound)**

4 tablespoons olive oil, divided

I zucchini, thinly sliced and quartered

**2 cups sliced oyster, shiitake, or crimini mushrooms
   (about 4 ounces)**

Salt and pepper to taste

Lemon wedges for garnish

Combine breadcrumbs, cheese, and parsley in shallow bowl. Reserve 3 tablespoons of crumb mixture. Place the egg in another shallow bowl. Dip pork chops first in egg, then in crumbs.

Heat 2 tablespoons of the olive oil in large nonstick skillet over moderate heat. Fry pork chops, in batches if necessary, about 3 to 4 minutes per side, just until opaque throughout. Transfer to a warm platter.

Wipe out skillet. Heat remaining 2 tablespoons olive oil over moderately high heat. Stir in zucchini and mushrooms and cook until mushrooms are tender and zucchini is crisp-tender, 4 to 5 minutes. Stir in reserved breadcrumb mixture and cook 1 minute longer. Season with salt and pepper to taste.

Place pork chop on plate next to zucchini-mushroom mixture and serve with lemon wedge. Makes 2 to 3 servings.

Turkey or Chicken
Cheddar-Crusted Potpie

I use up leftover barbecued chicken in this recipe. The smoky barbe-cue flavor penetrates the filling and adds another dimension to this old-fashioned pie.

CRUST

> 1 $^1/_2$ cups flour
>
> $^3/_4$ cup shredded cheddar cheese
>
> 8 tablespoons (1 stick) cold unsalted butter,
>   cut into small pieces
>
> 2 tablespoons vegetable shortening
>
> 5–8 tablespoons ice-cold water
>
> $^1/_4$ teaspoon salt

In food processor, add flour, cheddar cheese, butter, and shorten-ing. Pulse until well combined. Sprinkle water over top and pulse just until mixture begins to form a ball. Press into a ball, then pat into a disk. Cover with plastic wrap and refrigerate until chilled, about 30 minutes. Meanwhile, make filling.

FILLING

> 2 tablespoons butter
>
> 1 medium onion, chopped (about 1 $^1/_2$ cups)
>
> 2 carrots, peeled and sliced
>
> 8 ounces crimini or button mushrooms, quartered
>
> 2 garlic cloves, minced
>
> 1 teaspoon fresh chopped or $^1/_2$ teaspoon dried sage
>
> $^1/_4$ cup flour
>
> 1 $^3/_4$ cups turkey or chicken broth or stock
>
> 1 $^3/_4$ cups cooked turkey or chicken, diced
>
> 2 tablespoons chopped fresh parsley
>
> salt and pepper to taste

Preheat oven to 400 degrees. In large skillet over moderate heat, melt butter. Stir in onion, carrots, mushrooms, garlic, and sage. Cook until vegetables are tender, 6 to 8 minutes. Sprinkle flour over vegetables. Stir and cook 2 minutes longer. Whisk in broth and simmer until thickened, 3 to 4 minutes. Stir in cooked chicken or turkey and parsley. Season with salt and pepper. Let cool slightly.

Roll out half of chilled dough to a 12-inch circle, and line a 9-inch pie pan. Fill with turkey or chicken mixture. Roll out remaining dough into a $\frac{1}{8}$-inch-thick, 12-inch-diameter circle. Carefully place over filling. Decoratively crimp edges, and prick top with fork. Place pie on cookie sheet and bake in lower third of oven until crust is golden brown, 25 to 30 minutes. Serve warm from the oven. Makes 6 to 8 servings.

Time-saving shortcut

Substitute frozen piecrust for the cheddar crust.

A handful of sliced exotic mushrooms transforms a basic pasta dish.

Side Dishes

Fresh or dried mushrooms infuse a wonderful richness into starchy or grain-laden side dishes. More robust-tasting mushrooms, such as shiitake, maitake, portabella, and crimini, go better with stronger-tasting meats like lamb, beef, roasted chicken, or grilled chops. Sesame Barley Mushroom Medley is a nutty combination that holds up well and absorbs any extra juices when served alongside a dish such as the marinated Flank Steak with Grilled Vegetables and Mushrooms (page 56).

Some mushrooms are less meaty and more subtle, as in the recipe for Radicchio, Oyster Mushrooms, and White Beans, a summery salad, or Mushroom Vegetable Toss, with raw white mushrooms, kidney beans, and crunchy vegetables cascading with buttermilk dressing. Serve this as an alternative to potato salad at your next outdoor barbecue.

Enoki and beech mushrooms make excellent garnishes for summery side dishes. Sauté sliced pom pom mushrooms in butter, garlic, and wine, and present over rice or noodles for a quick and easy side dish.

Sesame Barley
Mushroom Medley

Grilled vegetables complement the rich nuttiness of this sesame-scented dish. If you can't find mushroom soy sauce, substitute regular soy sauce.

- 2 cups water
- 2 cups Beef Broth (page 97)
- $^3/_4$ cup barley
- I tablespoon sesame oil
- 2 tablespoons olive oil
- $^1/_2$ pound mixed mushrooms, such as crimini, button, portabella, shiitake, or maitake
- 2 garlic cloves, minced
- $^1/_2$ cup sliced scallions (about 3)
- I tablespoon mushroom soy sauce (page 102)
- I tablespoon sesame seeds

In medium saucepan, bring water and broth to boil. Stir in barley, cover, and reduce to simmer until liquid has been absorbed, 40 to 45 minutes.

In large skillet over moderate heat, heat sesame and olive oils. Stir in mushrooms and cook until softened and liquid has evaporated, about 5 minutes. Stir in garlic and scallions. Cook 1 minute longer. Remove from heat. Stir barley and soy sauce into mushroom mixture. Toast sesame seeds in a nonstick skillet over moderate heat until aromatic and golden, about 2 minutes. Sprinkle over mushrooms and barley and serve warm. Makes 4 servings.

Time-saving shortcut

Substitute canned beef broth for homemade.

Cheddar Mushroom Spaetzle

Spaetzle are German noodles or dumplings made with eggs, water or milk, and flour.

2 eggs
$^2/_3$ cup water
I tablespoon grainy mustard
$^1/_4$ teaspoon dried thyme
$^1/_2$ teaspoon salt
$^1/_8$ teaspoon pepper
I $^1/_3$ cups flour
2 tablespoons butter
2 cups sliced assorted mushroom caps, such as crimini, shiitake (stems removed), maitake, portabella, or white
$^1/_3$ cup sliced scallions
2 tablespoons sour cream
$^1/_2$ cup shredded cheddar cheese
3 slices cooked crisp bacon, crumbled

Preheat oven to 400 degrees. Bring large saucepan of water to boil.

In large bowl, whisk together eggs, water, mustard, thyme, salt, and pepper. Stir in flour until just combined. Scrape mixture into spaetzle maker set over saucepan. Using grating motion, drop spaetzle noodles into boiling water. (A wide-holed colander may be substituted for the spaetzle maker. Working in 3 batches, use a rubber spatula to press dough through holes into boiling water.) Allow each batch to float to the surface and continue to cook until firm, about 1 minute. Scoop out cooked spaetzle with a slotted spoon between batches. Drain and transfer to quart-size ovenproof or microwavable gratin dish or baking pan.

In medium skillet, melt butter. Stir in mushrooms and cook until softened and liquid is evaporated, about 5 minutes. Add scallions and cook 1 minute longer. Stir mushrooms and scallions into spaetzle. Stir in sour cream. Toss lightly with cheese and top with bacon. Bake in preheated oven until cheese is melted and spaetzle is heated through, about 6 minutes or cook in microwave 1 to 2 minutes until heated through. Makes 4 servings.

Spring Vegetable Mushrooms

Make this side dish in the spring, when fresh sugar snap peas are available.

> 8 ounces sugar snap peas (about 2 cups),
>   trimmed if necessary
>
> 1 1/2 cups fresh or frozen peas
>
> 1 teaspoon sugar
>
> 1 teaspoon cornstarch
>
> 1 tablespoon balsamic vinegar
>
> 1/3 cup Chicken Stock (page 96) or Beef Broth
>   (page 97)
>
> 2 tablespoons olive oil
>
> 4 ounces fresh mushrooms, such as crimini,
>   button, morel, or chanterelle
>
> salt and pepper to taste

In large saucepan, bring 2 quarts salted water to a boil. Add sugar snap peas and boil until crisp-tender, about 3 minutes. Using slotted spoon, transfer peas to a colander and refresh under cold running water. Transfer to medium bowl.

Add fresh or frozen peas to boiling water and cook until tender, about 2 minutes. Transfer peas to colander (you can dump out water now too) and refresh under cold running water. Toss into sugar snap peas and set aside.

In small bowl, stir together sugar, cornstarch, vinegar, and broth. Set aside.

In large frying pan or cast-iron skillet over moderate heat, heat olive oil. Add mushrooms and cook until tender, about 5 minutes. Carefully whisk in reserved broth mixture. Bring liquid to a boil. Reduce heat and simmer until thickened, about 1 minute. Toss peas into mushroom mixture, heat through, then scrape into serving dish. Season with salt and pepper. Serve warm or at room temperature. Makes 6 servings.

Wild Rice with Mushrooms and Roasted Peppers

Transform this recipe into a summer dish by tossing in $\frac{1}{2}$ cup feta cheese, 2 tablespoons balsamic vinegar, and 4 tablespoons extra virgin olive oil. Serve warm, at room temperature, or chilled on lettuce leaves.

- **4 tablespoons butter**
- **1 large onion, chopped**
- **2 garlic cloves, minced**
- **$\frac{3}{4}$ pound white or exotic mushrooms, such as crimini, shiitake, trumpet, or maitake, sliced**
- **1 teaspoon fresh crumbled or $\frac{1}{2}$ teaspoon dried oregano**
- **$\frac{1}{2}$ teaspoon salt**
- **$\frac{1}{8}$ teaspoon freshly ground pepper**
- **3 cups Chicken Stock (page 96) or water**
- **$\frac{3}{4}$ cup wild rice**
- **1 cup long-grain white rice**
- **1 red and 1 yellow bell pepper, roasted (page 102), peeled, and sliced into 1-by-$\frac{1}{8}$-inch pieces**
- **2 tablespoons chopped fresh Italian parsley**

In 3-quart skillet or saucepan, melt butter. Stir in onion, garlic, mushrooms, oregano, salt, and pepper. Cook until onions and mushrooms are tender, about 8 minutes. Scrape into bowl and set aside.

In same pan, bring chicken broth to boil. Stir in wild rice. Reduce heat, cover, and simmer for 30 minutes. Stir in long-grain rice, cover, and simmer for 20 to 25 minutes more, until both rices are tender. Remove from heat and stir in reserved mushroom mixture, peppers, and parsley. Adjust seasonings if necessary. Makes 8 to 10 servings.

Time-saving shortcuts

Substitute canned chicken broth for the homemade chicken stock. Roasted peppers can be found at the supermarket in jars or at the deli.

Roasted Rosemary Potatoes

These roasted potatoes remind me of the Swiss shredded potato pancake dish Rosti, which translates as "crisp and golden." These diced potatoes are cooked in a cast-iron skillet in a hot oven. The layer of mushrooms and cheese enriches this homey potato dish.

3 tablespoons butter, divided

1 small sweet yellow onion, thinly sliced

1 teaspoon sugar

$1/_2$ pound fresh shiitake mushroom caps, sliced, or maitake mushrooms, cleaned and coarsely chopped

2 pounds russet (baking) potatoes, peeled and cut into $1/_2$-inch dice

2 tablespoons olive oil

1 teaspoon dried rosemary

$1/_2$ teaspoon salt

$1/_4$ teaspoon freshly ground black pepper

1 cup shredded Gruyère or Swiss cheese (about 4 ounces)

Preheat oven to 425 degrees. In a 10-inch cast-iron skillet over moderate heat, melt 1 tablespoon of the butter. Add onion and sugar. Cover and cook until onion is soft, about 10 minutes. Remove cover and continue to cook onion slices until golden brown, about 5 minutes longer. Scrape into bowl and set aside.

In same skillet over moderate heat, melt remaining 2 tablespoons of butter. Cook mushrooms until tender, 5 to 6 minutes. Scrape into bowl with onions.

In same skillet, toss potatoes with olive oil, rosemary, salt, and pepper. Place skillet in center of preheated oven, and roast until potatoes are golden brown and tender, about 35 minutes. Remove from oven, and spread mushroom and onion mixture evenly over top. Sprinkle with cheese and return to oven. Cook until cheese is melted, about 10 minutes longer. Makes 6 servings.

Time-saving shortcut

Onions and mushrooms may be cooked a day in advance. Cover and refrigerate. Bring to room temperature before continuing.

Roasted Mushrooms and Pesto Pasta

This colorful pesto salad stands out on the buffet table. It makes a wonderful accompaniment to grilled seafood.

1 cup loosely packed basil leaves

$1/3$ cup loosely packed parsley or cilantro leaves

$1/2$ cup grated Parmesan cheese

9 tablespoons olive oil, divided

$1/2$ teaspoon salt

8 ounces mixed exotic mushrooms, such as shiitake, crimini, and oyster, sliced

$1/2$ pound penne pasta

1 cup diced tomatoes

$1/4$ cup toasted pine nuts (pignoli nuts)

salt and pepper to taste

Preheat oven to 400 degrees. In blender or food processor, pulse together basil, parsley or cilantro, Parmesan cheese, 6 tablespoons of the olive oil, and salt. Set aside.

Line large cookie sheet with foil. Scatter mushrooms over foil and toss gently with remaining 3 tablespoons of olive oil. Sprinkle mushrooms with salt and pepper to taste, and cover with another piece of foil. Roast mushrooms in oven until tender, 20 to 30 minutes.

Meanwhile, in large pot of boiling salted water, cook pasta until al dente. Drain well, transfer to large bowl, and toss with pesto mixture, roasted mushrooms, tomatoes, and pine nuts. Season to taste. Serve warm or at room temperature. Makes 8 to 10 servings.

Time-saving shortcut

Substitute $2/3$ cup store-bought pesto for basil-parsley mixture, and omit the first step of the recipe.

Brussels Sprouts and Crimini Mushroom Kabobs

When making kabobs, skewer vegetables together that require similar grilling times. By boiling Brussels sprouts first to crisp-tender, they may then be paired up with mushroom caps and finished off on the grill. Use this colorful combination of vegetables to accompany grilled steaks or chops.

> 1 tablespoon lemon juice
> 3 tablespoons extra-virgin olive oil
> $1/4$ teaspoon oregano
> $1/4$ teaspoon salt
> $1/8$ teaspoon freshly ground black pepper
> 10 ounces Brussels sprouts (about 19 sprouts)
> 8 ounces crimini mushrooms, stems trimmed
>   even with caps

Preheat grill. In small bowl, whisk together lemon juice, olive oil, oregano, salt, and pepper to make marinade. In medium saucepan, bring 2 quarts water to boil. Boil Brussels sprouts until crisp-tender, 7 to 8 minutes. Transfer to colander and refresh under cold running water. Drain well. Place in medium bowl. Toss with mushroom caps and marinade. Thread decoratively onto 4 metal skewers.

Grill skewers 3 to 4 minutes per side, until mushrooms are cooked through. Serve kabobs on skewers or slide off vegetables into serving dish. Makes 4 servings.

Time-saving shortcut

Substitute bottled vinaigrette dressing for lemon juice and olive oil marinade.

Tomato Mushroom
Polenta Pizza

Wedges of this vegetarian polenta pizza may be served as a first course, or add a tossed salad and garlic breadsticks and have it as a main course.

2 tablespoons butter or olive oil

I garlic clove, minced

I small onion, finely chopped

4 ounces shiitake, oyster, and crimini mushrooms, thinly sliced

3 tomatoes, peeled, seeded, and chopped

$^1/_4$ teaspoon oregano, crumbled

$^1/_4$ teaspoon salt

$^1/_8$ teaspoon pepper

I recipe Polenta (page 95)

$^3/_4$ cup shredded mozzarella cheese

Preheat oven to 400 degrees. In large skillet over moderate heat, heat butter or olive oil. Stir garlic and onion, and sauté until onion is softened, 5 to 6 minutes. Add mushrooms and cook about 5 minutes, until mushrooms are softened. Add tomatoes and seasonings. Cover and simmer until thickened, 25 to 30 minutes.

Spread tomato mushroom mixture over top of polenta. Sprinkle with cheese and bake in middle of oven for 15 minutes, or until cheese is melted and polenta is heated through. Makes 6 servings.

Time-saving shortcut

Substitute a 1-pound roll of store-bought polenta, found in the produce section. Cut into $^1/_2$-inch slices, and arrange in circle in 10-inch pie pan.

Grilled Portabella
Mushroom Slices

These mushroom slices may be served as an appetizer or as a side dish to grilled meats. For additional color and flavor, grill thick slices of red onion and toss into residual marinade with grilled mushroom slices.

> **2 large portabella mushrooms, stems removed**
> **2 tablespoons red wine vinegar**
> **$1/_3$ cup olive oil**
> **I garlic clove, minced**
> **$1/_2$ teaspoon chopped fresh or $1/_4$ teaspoon dried rosemary**
> **$1/_2$ teaspoon chopped fresh or $1/_4$ teaspoon crumbled**
>   **dried oregano**
> **I teaspoon Montreal Steak Seasoning**

Preheat grill. Wipe mushrooms clean with wet paper towel and cut into $1/_2$-inch slices. In glass baking pan, spread mushroom slices out. Whisk together remaining ingredients and pour over mushrooms. Let marinate 15 to 20 minutes. Grill about 2 minutes per side or until tender. Makes 2 servings.

Mushroom Vegetable Toss

Serve this colorful blend atop lettuce leaves. The combination makes a cool, light lunch for summer. Use rubber gloves when cutting jalapeños to avoid hands burning.

**2 cups white or crimini mushrooms,
  quartered**

**I green pepper, cut into $^1/_2$-inch pieces
  (about I cup)**

**I $^1/_2$ cups kidney beans (15 $^1/_2$-ounce can),
  rinsed and drained**

$^1/_2$ cup corn kernels

I medium carrot, grated

I small onion, finely diced

2 shallots, finely diced

I small jalapeño, minced

3 tablespoons lime juice

$^1/_2$ cup mayonnaise

$^1/_2$ cup buttermilk

$^1/_4$ teaspoon salt

$^1/_4$ teaspoon freshly ground black pepper

$^1/_2$ teaspoon ground cumin

3 tablespoons chopped fresh cilantro

In large bowl, mix together first 6 ingredients. In medium bowl, whisk together remaining ingredients to make dressing. Toss into vegetable mixture. Divide salad on 4 plates lined with beds of lettuce. Makes 4 servings.

Pearl Onions
and Mushrooms

My grandmother always made creamed onions for Thanksgiving. This recipe was a long, drawn-out process with numerous steps, including peeling all of those darned pearl onions. I've enhanced Granny's version by subtracting the labor-intensive pearl onion preparation and adding freshly sautéed mushrooms. You can make this yummy side dish in advance and refrigerate, then reheat in the microwave before serving.

By adding pasta and homemade Cream Sauce (page 98) or store-bought Alfredo sauce, you can turn this side dish into a main course. Toss sauce and some freshly shaved Parmesan cheese into your choice of pasta.

2 tablespoons butter

$1/_4$ pound mushrooms, such as crimini, beech, white, or royal trumpet, sliced (about 3 cups loosely packed)

1 9-ounce package frozen pearl onions in cream sauce, thawed

1 teaspoon chopped parsley

salt and pepper to taste

In medium skillet over moderate heat, melt butter. Add mushrooms and sauté until liquid evaporates, about 5 minutes. Stir in onions and parsley. Season with salt and pepper. Serve warm. Makes 4 to 6 servings.

Radicchio, Oyster Mushrooms, and White Beans

This side dish is lovely and light.

3 tablespoons olive oil, divided

I garlic clove, minced

2$^1/_2$ ounces oyster mushrooms, stems trimmed and caps sliced

3 cups shredded radicchio (about I small 5-ounce head)

$^1/_2$ cup canned northern white beans, rinsed and drained

I tablespoon chopped cilantro

I tablespoon lemon juice

$^1/_2$ teaspoon salt

$^1/_4$ teaspoon freshly ground pepper

In large skillet over moderate heat, heat 1 tablespoon of the olive oil. Stir in garlic and cook 1 minute. Sauté mushrooms until tender, about 5 minutes. Scrape out of skillet and set aside.

In same skillet, heat remaining 2 tablespoons of olive oil. Stir in radicchio and sauté until wilted, about 2 minutes. Stir in beans, cilantro, lemon juice, salt, pepper, and mushrooms. Heat through and serve. Makes 4 servings.

Raw, sliced white mushrooms perk up mixed greens.

Build-Ons and Add-Ons

This section includes some basic build-ons that are often needed for other recipes, as well as several add-ons, seasonings, and condiments that you can use to enhance mushroom dishes or to add a mushroom flavor to other dishes. Some of the build-on recipes can be made in advance and kept on hand in the refrigerator or freezer for use in other recipes in this book. Many of these recipes are for cooks who enjoy spending time in the kitchen making their own staples. If you're not one of those, or if you're pressed for time, store-bought items can often be substituted, such as canned beef or chicken broth, bottled vinaigrette, jars of roasted bell peppers, or rolls of polenta, which can be found in the produce section of most groceries. I prefer the taste of the homemade Cream Sauce, but you can substitute a 14-ounce jar of prepared Alfredo sauce in most recipes. If you have the time and the desire to make everything from scratch, here are the recipes. If not, time-saving shortcuts are offered throughout the book. Take off your apron and relax.

Duxelles
(Mushroom Filling)

This flexible mushroom mixture may be used for many recipes from appetizers to entrées, to stuff phyllo cups, spread on garlic toast, or swipe across chicken breasts before baking. The rich flavor of sautéed mushrooms permeates any dish.

I small onion, quartered

4 cups coarsely chopped mixed fresh mushrooms, such as white, crimini, shiitake (stems removed), oyster, and trumpet

3 tablespoons butter

2 garlic cloves, minced

I $\frac{1}{2}$ teaspoons lemon juice

$\frac{1}{2}$ teaspoon salt

$\frac{1}{4}$ teaspoon pepper

2 tablespoons chopped parsley

In food processor, chop onion. Scrap into small bowl. Add mushrooms to food processor, and pulse until coarsely chopped.

In large heavy skillet over moderately high heat, melt butter and stir in onion. Add mushrooms and garlic, and cook until liquid is evaporated and mixture stiffens, about 8 minutes. Remove from heat and stir in lemon juice, salt, pepper, and parsley. Makes 1$\frac{1}{4}$ cups.

Lemon Pesto Stuffing

The flavor of this stuffing permeates whatever meat you use it with. Use it to stuff whole roasting chickens, thick-cut butterflied pork chops, or Cornish hens. For extra flavor, make breadcrumbs from day-old crusty roasted-garlic loaf. Pesto is available at groceries or specialty food stores.

3 cups fresh breadcrumbs

$^1/_4$ cup pesto

2 tablespoons lemon juice

$^1/_4$–$^1/_2$ teaspoon salt (vary depending on saltiness of pesto)

$^1/_4$ teaspoon freshly ground black pepper

5 tablespoons butter, divided

I medium yellow onion, finely chopped

I celery stalk, finely chopped

I carrot, finely chopped

3 cups white or mix of exotic mushrooms, such as shiitake, trumpet, oyster, portabella, crimini, or beech (stems trimmed), coarsely chopped

$^1/_4$ cup toasted pine nuts (optional)

In food processor, pulse breadcrumbs, pesto, lemon juice, salt, and pepper, until combined. Scrape into large bowl.

In large skillet over moderate heat, melt 3 tablespoons of the butter. Stir in onion, celery, and carrot. Cook until vegetables are softened, about 6 to 8 minutes. Scrape into bowl with breadcrumb mixture.

In same skillet, melt remaining 2 tablespoons of butter. Sauté mushrooms until softened and liquid is evaporated, about 5 minutes. Scrape into breadcrumbs and toss until well combined. Stir in pine nuts, if desired. Makes 5 cups.

Time-saving shortcuts

To speed up the preparation, chop onion, carrot, and celery in food processor.

Purchase fresh breadcrumbs or breadcrumbs for stuffing at the supermarket.

Parmesan Pepper Focaccia

As a variation, arrange sautéed exotic mushrooms over top of focaccia dough, sprinkle with cheese, drizzle with olive oil, and bake.

1 1/4 cups warm water, divided
1 package dry active yeast (a scant tablespoon)
2 teaspoons honey or sugar
3 tablespoons olive oil, divided
2 1/4–2 1/2 cups flour
1 teaspoon salt
cracked pepper
1/4 cup shredded Parmesan cheese

In small bowl, combine 1/4 cup water, yeast, and honey or sugar. Let sit until foamy, about 10 minutes. In medium bowl, place remaining 1 cup of water, and stir in 2 tablespoons of the olive oil and the yeast mixture. Mix in flour and salt. Knead until smooth and elastic. Place dough in oiled bowl. Cover and let double in bulk, about 2 hours. Punch down dough, then pat into 10-inch greased glass pie pan. Cover and let rise about 30 minutes.

Preheat oven to 400 degrees. Brush top of dough with remaining 1 tablespoon of oil. Crack pepper over top of dough, and sprinkle with Parmesan cheese. Bake in center of oven for 25 to 30 minutes, until golden brown. Makes 8 wedges.

Polenta

This cornmeal mush mixture is available in the produce section of the grocery in rolls, but it's easy—and much less expensive—to whip up your own polenta. This recipe calls for Parmesan cheese, but you can substitute Gorgonzola or Asiago. Fresh or dried herbs and sautéed mushrooms may be incorporated to enhance the flavor.

$1/_2$ cup yellow cornmeal
$1/_2$ teaspoon salt
$2^1/_2$ cups Chicken Stock (page 96)
$1/_3$ cup Parmesan cheese
1 tablespoon butter

In medium bowl, stir together cornmeal, salt, and 1 cup of broth or water. In 1-quart saucepan, bring remaining $1\frac{1}{2}$ cups of broth or water to a boil. Whisking constantly, slowly pour cornmeal into boiling water. Reduce heat to simmer and cook, whisking, until very thick, 30 to 35 minutes. Remove from heat and stir in Parmesan cheese and butter. Spread evenly in a greased 10-inch pie pan. You may cover and refrigerate polenta for up to 6 days. Makes 6 servings.

Time-saving shortcut

Substitute canned chicken broth or water for stock.

Chicken Stock

You can accumulate chicken bones and leftover pieces in your freezer to throw into the stockpot, or you can use a roaster carcass after picking off most of the meat. Leftover onions or leeks, mushrooms, tomatoes, and peppers may all be tossed in the pot for added flavor. Freeze stock in usable increments, such as 2-cup plastic containers, or freeze in ice cube trays, pop out, and place in Ziploc bags.

5 pounds chicken bones, pieces, or raw backs and necks
I medium onion, peeled and quartered
I medium carrot, peeled and coarsely chopped
3 garlic cloves, smashed
I bay leaf
I teaspoon black peppercorns
2 parsley sprigs

In 4-quart stockpot or large saucepan, place chicken bones, pieces, or carcass, and pour in enough water to cover by 1 inch, about 3 quarts. Add remaining ingredients. Bring water just to a boil. Skim any foamy impurities off surface, reduce heat, and simmer for 2 to 3 hours. Strain. Refrigerate, then skim off any hardened fat on surface. Makes 2 quarts.

Beef Broth

Store broth in 2-cup containers in the freezer. You can also freeze broth in ice cube trays, then transfer frozen cubes to plastic freezer bags.

4 pounds beef bones with marrow
I yellow onion, peeled and quartered
$^1/_2$ cup mushroom stems or pieces (optional)
I carrot, peeled and cut into 3-inch length
2 celery stalks, cut into 3-inch lengths
3 garlic cloves, unpeeled
16 cups cold water

Preheat oven to 450 degrees. Roast beef bones in large ovenproof casserole for 20 minutes. Add onion, mushrooms, carrot, celery, and garlic and roast until softened, another 50 to 60 minutes. Or, put bones, vegetables, mushrooms, and pan scrapings into 5-quart saucepan, and add water. Bring liquid to a boil, skimming occasionally. Reduce heat and simmer 2 to $2^1/_2$ hours. Strain. Makes 2 quarts.

Cream Sauce

For a quick pasta dinner, stir sautéed mushrooms and crisp-tender vegetables into your favorite cooked noodles. Toss in Cream Sauce and grated Parmesan cheese. You can make a lighter version of this sauce by changing the proportions slightly, using 1 cup chicken broth and $\frac{1}{2}$ cup heavy cream. If too thick, thin with additional liquid.

2 tablespoons butter
2 tablespoons flour
$\frac{1}{2}$ cup Chicken Stock (page 96)
or canned chicken broth
1 cup heavy cream
$\frac{1}{4}$ teaspoon salt
pinch nutmeg

In heavy saucepan or top of double boiler over moderate heat, melt butter. Whisk in flour and cook until mixture and foamy. Whisking constantly, stir in chicken broth, cream, salt, and nutmeg. Bring to a boil and simmer, stirring, until thickened, 3 to 5 minutes. Makes about 2 cups.

Vermouth
Mushroom Sauce

This sauce is delicious over grilled chicken or veal chops. Try incorporating different mushrooms in the sauce, such as oyster, crimini, trumpet, maitake, or pom pom. For a lighter, tangier sauce, omit the cream. Garnish with chopped fresh parsley, cilantro, snipped chives, or fresh thyme leaves.

  1 tablespoon butter

  1 tablespoon olive oil

  3 large shallots, minced

  3 garlic cloves, minced

  3 cups thinly sliced exotic
     or white mushrooms

  $1/2$ cup vermouth

  $2^1/3$ cups Chicken Stock (page 96)

  2 tablespoons cornstarch

  1 tablespoon lemon juice

  1 tablespoon water

  $1/3$ cup heavy cream

  1 teaspoon fresh thyme
     or $1/2$ teaspoon dried

  salt and pepper to taste

In 2-quart saucepan over moderately high heat, heat butter and oil. Add shallots, garlic, and mushrooms, and cook until liquid evaporates, 4 to 5 minutes. Stir in vermouth, bring liquid to a boil, and simmer until reduced by half, about 2 minutes. Add chicken broth and bring back to a boil.

In small cup, dissolve cornstarch in lemon juice and water. Whisk into sauce. Stir in cream, along with thyme, and boil until slightly thickened, about 1 minute. Season to taste with salt and pepper. Makes $3^1/4$ cups.

Time-saving shortcut

Substitute canned chicken broth for homemade stock.

Mushroom Herb Sauce

Spoon this sauce over grilled chops, chicken, or steak.

I tablespoon butter

I tablespoon olive oil

$^1/_2$ cup finely chopped onion

3 cups white or crimini mushrooms, quartered
(about 12 ounces)

2 garlic cloves, minced

I tablespoon fresh or $1^1/_2$ teaspoons dried tarragon

$^1/_3$ cup dry red wine

$1^2/_3$ cups Beef Broth (page 97)

$^3/_4$ cup plus I tablespoon water

2 teaspoons red wine vinegar

$2^1/_2$ tablespoons cornstarch

2 tablespoons chopped fresh parsley

In large saucepan over moderately high heat, heat butter and olive oil. Stir in onion and cook until softened, 5 to 6 minutes. Stir in mushrooms and sauté until slightly golden, 4 to 5 minutes. Add garlic and cook 1 minute longer. Stir in tarragon and red wine. Simmer until liquid is reduced by half, about 2 minutes. Stir in beef broth and $^3/_4$ cup water. Bring to a boil and simmer for 2 minutes.

In small cup, combine 1 tablespoon cold water, vinegar, and cornstarch until smooth. Whisk into sauce. Bring back to a boil and cook until slightly thickened, about 1 minute. Stir in parsley. Makes 4 cups.

Time-saving shortcut

Substitute a $13^3/_4$-ounce can of beef broth for homemade.

Creamy Morel Mushroom Sauce

As a main course, pour this sauce over veal or pork scallopini. For an elegant appetizer, stir in a handful of cooked shrimp and some sliced green onions, and spoon into baked pastry shells.

1 tablespoon butter
1 large shallot, minced
$1/3$ cup morels, washed and larger caps halved
2 tablespoons calvados (optional)
$1/2$ cup chicken broth
3 tablespoons heavy cream
salt and pepper to taste

In medium skillet, melt butter. Add shallot and morels and cook until softened, 2 to 3 minutes. Stir in calvados, if desired, and simmer until liquid is reduced by half. Stir in chicken broth and again reduce by half. Add cream and bring just to a boil. Season with salt and pepper. Makes $3/4$ cup.

Vinaigrette Marinade

Brush this marinade over mushroom caps before grilling or baking.

1 tablespoon Dijon mustard
1 garlic clove, minced
2 tablespoons white wine vinegar
1 tablespoon chopped parsley
$1/4$ teaspoon salt
$1/2$ teaspoon sugar
$1/8$ teaspoon freshly ground black pepper
6 tablespoons olive oil

In small bowl, whisk together all ingredients. Makes about $1/2$ cup.

Roasted Bell Peppers

If using a gas range, set peppers directly over flame on rack above burner and char the outer skin completely, turning with tongs. If you don't have a gas range, preheat broiler, and broil peppers on a cookie sheet close to the heat source until outer skin is charred all over.

Using tongs, place charred peppers in paper bag and let sit for 10 minutes. Then rinse peppers under cold running water over a colander and peel off charred outer skin. Remove seeds and ribs, and slice to desired thickness.

Roasted Mushrooms

Preheat the oven to 400 degrees. Line a large cookie sheet with aluminum foil, and spray with vegetable or olive oil spray. Scatter $^3/_4$ pound cleaned and sliced mushrooms. (Portabellas, shiitakes, and criminis all work well, but cut them into same-size slices so they will cook evenly in the oven without burning.) Spray or drizzle with oil, and sprinkle with salt, pepper, and perhaps a little dried herb such as thyme, rosemary, or basil. Cover mushrooms with another piece of foil, and roast in the oven for 30 to 40 minutes, until mushrooms are tender. These roasted mushroom slices can be eaten as a snack or sprinkled over soups, salads, or sautéed vegetables as a garnish.

Mushroom Soy Sauce

Available at Asian food markets, this aromatic mushroom-steeped soy sauce can be used to enrich stir-fries, grilled fish and pork, marinades, or dipping sauces.

Frozen Mushrooms

The best way to freeze mushrooms is to first slice them and sauté in butter or oil. Then spread the sautéed mushrooms out on a cookie sheet or tray that will fit in the freezer, and freeze until the mushrooms are firm. Transfer frozen mushrooms to Ziploc bags labeled by mushroom variety. Frozen sautéed mushrooms may be used straight from freezer to recipe; they are cooked and ready to use. Fresh frozen mushrooms tend to get soggy and limp, but they can be used to enhance the flavor of soups or stocks.

Mushroom Butter

Grind dried mushrooms in a clean coffee grinder until powdery. Combine 2 tablespoons of mushroom powder with 1 stick of softened butter. Roll up in waxed paper or plastic wrap and freeze. When ready to use, slice off butter by the tablespoon. Return unused quantity to the freezer. This butter is great melted over grilled chops or fish fillets. Slip under the skin of a roasting chicken or toss into pasta for a quick flavor lift.

Mushroom Seasoning Mixes

Grind dried mushrooms such as porcinis, shiitakes, or chanterelles in a clean coffee grinder. Combine this mushroom powder with dried herbs or spices, toasted sesame seeds, and Parmesan cheese to create unique seasoning mixes.

Truffle-Scented Oil

The flavor of these highly concentrated oils comes from an infusion of black or white truffle aroma. Mushroom-infused oils are becoming much more visible in gourmet food shops, as well as in the pasta and tomato sauce aisles of the local supermarket. Agribosco and Urbani are two good brands to use. Truffle oil is also easy to make at home. Simply chop several slices of truffle finely and add to a mild-tasting oil such as light olive oil or grapeseed oil. The more surface of the truffle that is exposed, the more flavorful the oil. Store jars of truffle oil in a cool, dark location, refrigerator, or freezer. A little dribble of truffle oil can transform the intensity of a dish. Use a few drops of oil at the end of cooking to flavor risotto, grilled meats, or sautéed vegetables, or to highlight salads and soups. A small droplet of truffle oil will go a long way to flavor appetizer or entrée, so don't use too much. The flavor is quite intense.

Sources

Basciani Foods, Inc.
944 Penn Green Rd.
Avondale, PA 19311
phone: 610-268-3610
open daily for fresh mushroom sales, 6 A.M.–6 P.M.

Bridge Kitchenware
Phone: 800-274-3435
www.bridgekitchenware.com
spaetzle maker

Country Fresh Mushroom Company
P.O. Box 489
Avondale, Pennsylvania 19311
phone: 610-268-3033, 800-253-6607
contact: Mike Reed
e-mail: Mreedcfmush@aol.com

Cutone
Routes 1 and 41
Avondale, PA 19311
phone: 610-268-2271
open daily for fresh mushroom sales, 8 A.M.–3 P.M.

Gourmet Mushroom Products
P.O. Box 515 IP
Graton, California 95444
phone: 707-829-7301, 800-789-9121
fax: 707-823-9091
www.gmushrooms.com
*gourmet mushroom oils, fresh and dried
mushrooms, mushroom growing kits*

La Espanola
phone: 310-539-0455
www.laespanolameats.com
black truffles, $6.95 for 10 grams

Mushroom Festival (beginning of September)
phone: 610-925-3373, 888-440-9920
www.mushroomfest.com

Mushroom Information Center
35 East 21st Street, 10th floor
New York, NY 10010
phone: 212-420-8808
e-mail: I-n@mushroominfo.com
www.mushroominfo.com

Phillips Mushroom Farms
1011 Kaolin Rd.
Kennett Square, PA 19348
phone: 800-722-8818
fax: 610-444-4751
www.phillipsmushroomfarms.com

Sher-rockee
170 SherRockee Lane
Lincoln University, PA 19352
phone: 610-869-8048
www.sherrockmush.com
open daily for fresh mushroom sales, 8 A.M.–4 P.M.

Shiitake-Ya
P.O. Box 7107
Huntington Beach, CA 92615-7101
www.shiitakeya.com
shiitake products, dried porcinis

www.cooking.com
stainless steel truffle cutter, about $15

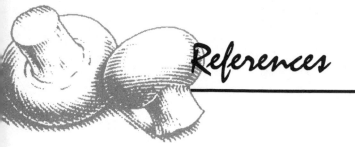

References

Books

Herbst, Sharon Tyler. *The New Food Lover's Companion.* 3rd ed. New York: Barron's Educational Series, 2001.

Konemann, Ludwig. *Culinaria European Specialties.* Vols. 1 and 2. Cologne: Verlagsgesellschaft mbH, 1995.

Persson, Olle. *The Chanterelle Book.* Berkeley, CA: Ten Speed Press, 1997.

Websites

http://www.mushroominfo.com/history/ami.html
Mushrooms—industry growth; development of the American Mushroom Industry (AMI).

www.mushroominfo.com/nutrition/minerals.html
Mushroom nutrition and minerals.

Index